LEARN TO MEDITATE IN 2 MINUTES

FOR THE LAZY, CRAZY AND TIME DEFICIENT

SHEEVAUN MORAN

PUBLISHED BY FASTPENCIL, INC.

Published by FastPencil, Inc.
3131 Bascom Ave.
Suite 150
Campbell CA 95008 USA
(408) 540-7571
(408) 540-7572 (Fax)
info@fastpencil.com
http://www.fastpencil.com

You can practice some of these techniques while driving, however for the more complicated ones please do not practice while driving.

First Edition

Acknowledgements

I'd like to acknowledge my teachers who have given me the inspiration to share this work. I gratefully thank the corporate environs for giving me the stress to find a way to help others out of their stress, pain and depression. I am immensely grateful for the students who have taken the steps to learn these techniques and telling me that you still use them today after many years, you are each creating a better world to live in.

CONTENTS

DEDICATION

To all my teachers for your faith that I could share
and to the students who inspired me to share what I know.

Atma Namaste!

Preface: Introduction

Simplicity simply accomplishes results.

I was speaking with someone about this book and told them the title. Their comment was "Wow, only two minutes? That's not enough. I used to do TM (Transcendental Meditation – a meditation technique taught to many thousands of people in the late '70s) for 60 minutes."

"What happened," I asked. "I got away from it because I couldn't find the time," she explained.

So this book is for everyone, those of us who are lazy, going crazy and those who don't have time, even a more seasoned meditation practitioner.

I have discovered through many classes, teaching busy executives, moms, entrepreneurs, and personal interactions that everyone has at least TWO minutes for meditation.

How about you?

After someone has taken my class, I often hear, "I have to go medicate, I mean meditate."

Interesting how the words medicate and meditate are interchangeable in our language. For many, medication is necessary to gain freedom from an ailment, while meditation can allow freedom from a physical, mental, or emotional ailment by allowing the body to achieve better balance and overall peace. Having a deeper peace allows the body to have less stress which results in better health.

For many years, I had heard of meditation, but I also had no *real* idea what it was or how to do it or if it was something that I needed. I grew up in a woodsy suburban area and I escaped into nature when I needed a break. Later, I learned that this was a form of meditation. After moving to the city, I knew I needed something to relieve life's stress so I tried lots of things - retreats with Jesuit Priests, hiking, exotic vacations, or just sitting to quiet my mind. Discovering that these attempts were ineffective, and only seemed to make matters worse, I surprisingly filled up my already busy schedule with more stuff.

I filled every ounce of my day with work, exercise, and everything else otherwise distracting to avoid having to slow down, rest and stop. To avoid the necessary rest, I even read books while working out on a stair climber, which only increased the chatter in my head. Similar to most people who have not learned to still the mind and to give it rest, I continued to overtax my brain and increase the tension in my mind and body. I followed the "more is better" axiom. Can you relate?

Also, similar to most people, I searched for countless things to bring me peace before I began to practice meditation. I took art classes and even thourgh I was good at it and loved it; the search to find peace still seemed to escape me. Drawing, painting, singing, although creative interests, stimulated the mind even more. I was not getting the feeling of peace and life became increasingly intense. As with most people, the more than 100 different ways in which I had tried to discover calm and peace were fleeting and did not work. When I got sick from loving my job and too many hours of work, I was ordered by my doctor to make a change for my mind and body. My doctor recommended meditation as a way to relieve stress, which would help to heal my sick and tired body. Not knowing how to rest, thinking of meditation only stressed me out more. In spite of my doctor recommendations, I continued the 16-hour days at work which included spending more than 80 percent of my time traveling. Similar to many people today, I was over-committed to my job and completely under-committed to living. The hectic travel schedule and intense pace was taking its toll.

Knowing that my body was still lacking rest and health, I decided to ignore the doctor, and found myself in the emergency room. I had acquired an infection that had poisoned my blood, leaving me on bed rest for a few weeks. I was 33 years old; however, from the prescribed treatment - rest, diet change, less travel, relaxation and meditation - I was apparently living with a body that was much older. The infection resulted in near death, which became the catalyst for finding a new way to live. I resolved to achieve more balance, no matter what I was involved with and, particularly in a working environment.

Having no real idea where to start I then tried regular massage, which helped to some small degree, but the underlying problem was still the same. I needed more inner peace and inner rest. It was about that time when I heard a radio host talking about how energy follows thought and intention and how it helps the body heal much faster. The guest on the radio shared a meditation and I felt some peace for the first time. All of a sudden it made sense.

Taking an alternative healing class, which was a pole apart from my career path in the pharmaceutical industry, I was again told to meditate. I had a good internal laugh. I started off with a few physical exercises, then sat down and closed my eyes, and listened to the meditation CD. After heckling the concept, I realized it was the first time I had fewer than one million thoughts racing through my mind.

Having been intrigued by this rare moment of quiet, I was hooked. Having purchased this miraculous meditation CD, I decided that I liked feeling happy and that I would begin to meditate on a regular basis. At the start, I practiced meditation two times a week as an experiment. Every time it was a discovery of finding more happiness and connecting with my true "happy" self. I took my meditation act on my business trips and wouldn't start my day without at least 20 minutes of practice. I soon discovered the many benefits of meditation, which included changes to my physical body and success in business. I found that my business deals closed easily, my body was feeling more at ease, and I had more free time and energy, despite having the same responsibilities and more clients. Similar to many people who begin a regular meditation practice, it soon became a way of life for me - I was wholeheartedly hooked.

While still working in the pharmaceutical industry, a client I was working with asked me to substitute as the teacher for her meditation class. Although I believed I was under qualified for such an endeavor, my client disagreed and said that she had learned meditation from me. I agreed to help her out and then she could go back to teaching the class.(I maintain that the best way to learn anything is to teach it to others.) During the first class, I realized the number of people who want to learn to meditate, but also, the amount of frustration that takes place in the process and practice of meditation. Experiencing my own frustration about how to actually meditate is where I started. Experiencing meditation as a foreign practice, I possessed a certain understanding—other people probably have similar feelings about the thought and practice of meditation. As I started the first meditation class that I had ever taught, I began by telling the students my story. It continues to be told to many students of meditation.

Since that first class, and my tenure as a meditation teacher at community colleges in Orange County, California, I have continued to expand my teachings to thousands of students throughout the United States and overseas.

* * *

A book that teaches meditation practices to others has been manifesting in my mind for quite sometime. Over the past several years, I have taught thousands of people from all walks of life to meditate. More than 89 percent of the students I have taught were first-timers. And similar to myself, each student wanted some type of peace in their life. Students who had meditated before wanted to learn new techniques to quiet their mind and to take their practices to the next level to reach even greater peace.

The idea for this practical meditation book began to take shape after several students recognized the affect of peace that my teachings and practices had on their lives. Even the students that told me that they could never learn to meditate have had success implementing my meditation practices. The success of these doubtful students, and many others, is easily attributable to my determination to break down the aspects of meditation in simple and practical steps.

Today, most people are consumed by the stress of contemporary life and are looking to reduce those pressures. Some reduce stress through alcohol, smoking, exercise, eating and yet none fo those methods will feed the need for a quiet mind or greater inner peace. Meditation is one of the easiest ways to reduce stress, yet it is also one of the most difficult practices to incorporate into our hectic and busy lives. Let's face it, we are overwhelmed with a multitude of responsibilities that include family, friends, careers and education to name a few. Applying the techniques shared in this book will allow meditation into your life. In all its simplicity, this book and its meditation teachings, reflect the personal experience of myself, and thousands of my students and their shift in consciousness from chaotic to calm. In taking the time to follow the techniques in this book, the possibility for less stress and more balanced life is easily created. These meditation techniques are so effective - embodying peace of mind, balance and happiness - that it's possible to put some of them into practice while you're reading this book, in two minutes or less. Moreover, with these meditation teachings and techniques, "simplicity simply accomplishes results" You will find that these techniques will take you through to the first steps and more deeply into the next steps in your meditation practice.

1

THE MYTH OF MEDITATION

*"Think of meditation as a log you throw
on to the fire of the soul. If you feed the
fire, you feed the soul. You connect to
the source and you create inner peace."*

~Sheevaun Moran

Can I really meditate without having a completely quiet mind?
Can I really meditate without sitting in a twisted position?
Can I meditate and not feel cultish?
Do I have to stare at a wall to meditate?
Can I meditate every so often?
Don't I need a teacher to start?

Imagine laying in the hospital with the doctor telling you that
your blood is poisoned and that you have to stay there for several
weeks. The doctor has told you that blood poisoning is lethal and
that you could die if something in your life didn't change.

Well that's exactly what happened to me. The body and brain would only take so much abuse. I had been stressing it out, not feeding it good food, not caring if I stayed
out late, not taking care of how much sleep I got, not interested in the fact that 16 hour work days had a price.

I had been told to learn to meditate and I had been told to get more rest. I had also been told that I needed to eat better and drink more water. Like so many others, I tried that for a few days and went back to an intense travel schedule and other bad habits.

Even after surgery to correct a misdiagnosis, I went back to my hectic schedule. That's when the body rebelled and I landed in the hospital.

Let me take you back to where and how I went from a quiet rural country girl to becoming a meditation teacher.

Imagine sitting by the side of a creek staring at the water without notice of time or place. Watch as the water dances and plays around the rocks and as it ebbs and flows along the creek side. Listen as the water makes slight gurgling. Feel your shoulders relax and just stare at the moving water.

As a young girl and into my adult life, I often found myself sitting by my favorite creek watching the water flow along the banks of the earth and over rocks. Little did I know, I was experiencing a form of meditation, also known as prolonged awareness, and I have been doing it most of my life.

Far removed from this image of the creek and the experience of prolonged awareness, I had formed a different image and belief of what meditation was about and how difficult it was. I associated meditation with the image of Hindu yogis in strange clothing, Buddhist yogis with orange robes and yellow hats, priests and nuns walking around without ever speaking, and the white robed Hare Krishna people promoting their faith at airports. I imagined yogis sitting in a lotus posture (a twisted position), using strange hand gestures (mudras) and alternately chanting unintelligible sounds or mantras (commonly repeated thoughts) and the need for complete quiet and stillness. My uneducated beliefs had most of these meditating people sequestered away from the world high on a mountaintop in the freezing climate with little or no contact with the outside world. I also thought that I'd need to stare at a wall for hours on end to succeed at meditation. I, like most people, had judged these images of meditation and yet knew that it would help me. These are only some of the mainstream myths and misconceptions of meditation.

Even the word meditation conjures up different images for each of us. Many people think of things that are weird or unfamiliar and unaccepted. Some religious practices think that meditation is against their rules and against their God. Meditation can also seem scary because it creates huge expectations, the weight and fear of impossibility. The most common thread that the word meditation brings up is the need for a completely quiet mind. Then there's the thought that if you meditate you're subject to the whim of a fanatic or other unscrupulous people, especially if one is meditating in a group. So much so that people who have never practiced meditation regularly believe that it's a cult practice, where one loses all control.

Adding to our own confusion is the onslaught of meditation books and CDs; major articles in health and wellness magazines; and fitness facilities teaching meditation. They claim that an individual must sit still in a twisted position for a long period of time to meditate. They must invest a lot of money per week in large classes.

What are your myths and misconceptions about meditation?

These are many of the myths of meditation:

too boring and I'm too busy

twisted sitting position

chanting strange words is required

the need to discard your own beliefs

succumb to the whim of others
must wear strange clothes
giving up the pleasures of life
staring at a blank wall
unless you meditate for an hour a day then it's not meditating
that only people who do yoga do meditation
that it will take years to do meditation right
lying down is meditating
I have to be spiritual to meditate
I'll be enlightened when I meditate
I'll give up all my friends who don't meditate
a completely quiet mind is required to meditate
my religion won't allow me to meditate, and
my favorite – I'm not like *those* people, I may need it but I'm not like that

I am here to tell you that these meditation myths are simply not true. Not only are the myths about meditation not true, they're completely impractical. Our busy lifestyle and diverse cultures create a great need for meditation.

Again, the word meditation brings up quite a few strange images that are accompanied by odd beliefs and feelings. Some include confusion, but most resemble fear. Fear of the unknown and fear of the weird. For most people (of all religions and spiritual backgrounds), the unknown is definitely something to fear. Many of my students, as well as myself, have shared similar feelings of confusion and fear before practicing meditation regularly. For me, one of meditation practices I had seen in the media projected the image of Buddhists who practice the form of Zen meditation.It is a form of meditation that tries to get you to empty your mind and attain mindfulness. This practice may be beneficial for some, but for the beginner it can be daunting. Zen instructs you to sit in front of an empty white wall and stay there until your mind has emptiness. This is nearly impossible for most people. In today's world, we have so many responsibilities that limits our time and our ability to have a completely quiet mind.

In the following examples, students who thought they couldn't meditate, share their experiences:

1. A student new to meditation thought it was nothing more than just sitting, which to her meant meditation was a passive and sedentary activity. With her busy schedule, she did not have time to "just sit there." Although meditation had been recommended to improve her health and overall well-being, she did not see the point and continued to believe meditation to be a waste of time rather than a practice that allows one to have greater awareness, and act more wisely and skillfully in the world. After learning to meditate and using my techniques, she has found happiness and peace in all areas of her life.

2. Another student believed that the objective of meditation was to have a quiet mind with no thoughts of what today, tomorrow or the next day's to-do-list demanded. She thought she needed to give up everything to dedicate herself to meditation in order for it to work. There is no such thing as a completely quiet mind. With meditation, the mind begins to shift its awareness from mundane tasks to a greater awareness, which brings less stress and more peace to your life. This does take some practice.

Students who had already done some form of meditation share their early ideas of meditation:

1. One student, an engineer, said his initial image of meditation was that of an Indian yogi (one who practices meditation for spiritual insight). Although he related the image to peace somehow, he had no desire to research the reality of meditation. His image remained as that of a yogi sitting lotus style

using strange hand gestures or mudras. Once we shared some simple techniques that gelled with his logical brain and how it related to peace, he became one of the most avid and dedicated students to meditation.

2. Another, more advanced student, who gave up complicated meditation techniques because she just didn't feel at peace, said that at first she thought meditation was something for priests or people of religion; and yet another shared that meditation for her invoked the image of the Hare Krishna (a group that engages in devotional chants to the Hindu god Krishna). She imagined the Hare Krishna in their brightly orange-colored robes at the airport chanting something she couldn't understand until much later: Hare/ Hare Rama, Hare Rama, Rama Rama, Hare Hare, which to the Hare Krishna invokes Krishna consciousness.

3. One student, a corporate big wig, shared that meditation was something intangible and ethereal. Although meditation practice was something he contemplated, he maintained the idea that if things were not concrete or earthly, he didn't think they had any value. Since meditation was something that was unfamiliar to him, he did not believe in it. He now meditates two times a day.

4. At the opposite extreme, another student shared that meditation was an adventure where you had to travel to remote places. It was also only for rich people.

5. Another student shared that she witnessed people paying $200 for a mantra (a spiritual thought form), which really turned her off meditation for 20 years, until she started my meditation class.

6. And yet another student, a mom with five kids, admitted that it was something she could never be a part of—meditation was something cultish or countercultural, and not prominent in the

United States. Now she has her children meditating with her and her household is much more peaceful.

Despite these myths and misconceptions, meditation can change every facet of your life. As a teacher of meditation for 15 years, I have witnessed the life enhancing effects in thousands of students. I, too, have seen and continue to see the benefits of meditation in all aspects of my life.

I give you permission right here, right now to allow yourself to delve into this strange and different, yet also extremely valuable, world that involves meditation.

Now that we've dispelled and de-mystified the image and idea of meditation, let's step back and look at the definition of the word meditation. Merriam Webster's dictionary defines meditation as "prolonged awareness". Prolonged awareness seems easier to understand because we have all experienced prolonged awareness. Yes, each and every one of you has experienced instances of prolonged awareness.

Have you ever driven home from work and didn't remember all of the details of how you got there? That is prolonged awareness. Who knows what you were aware of, but likely, it wasn't the road. Have you ever read a page in a book, then turned to the next page, suddenly realizing you had to go back several pages because you didn't recall what you had read? That too, is considered prolonged awareness. When you lose track of time because you're so involved in your work and you suddenly notice that hours have gone by, that's prolonged awareness (meditation). If you have ever been so engaged in your project, performance, presentation, conversation that you have been unaware of anyone trying to get your attention, know that those are all forms of prolonged awareness.

Some people may laugh at these examples, claiming it is just spacing out or zoning out. Actually zoning out is a form of meditation. It may be meditation lite, but never the less a form. Whether driving or reading a book, the brain is aware and functioning, yet it is also taking a rest from the task at hand. In other words, while taking a rest from the mundane routines of driving or reading, the brain is engaged in a form of prolonged awareness.

The fact is, our brains need a break from routine, from the constant hum of daily activities, and from the constant onslaught of input. These breaks or prolonged awareness come to people in many different forms, however, these bouts of prolonged awareness do come to each and every one of us daily. It is estimated, that we have an episode of prolonged awareness every 15 minutes. Meditation, which is prolonged awareness, becomes a question of subject matter—how and what are you being aware of in order to meditate?

So now that my students and I have dispelled the common myths of meditation, let me share some of their success stories.

Just because the word "meditation" may give you concern, don't let the opportunity pass you by. You may be passing up the chance to reward yourself with good health, happiness and peace.

Skip to Chapters 10 and 14 if you are ready to start, and bypass all the foundational information.

❋ One student shared that practicing meditation allows him to tap into the rhythm of life in a more direct way.

❋ Another student who had a drug and alcohol addiction shared that meditation is much better than any dope she ever did—that it really gives her the inner peace she was always searching for when she was using.

❋ One student said meditation gives her a way to deal with the world and the craziness of people more productively. She is able to bring prolonged awareness into every moment of her life, which directs her life more consciously rather than unconsciously.

❋ Another student shared that since she began to meditate regularly miraculous things have happened in her life; however more importantly, she had learned that meditation is so much about service to others in the world and not just inner reflection.

❋ One student shared that meditation is a great healing and centering tool—it is an instrument of healing for him, as well as others. In this way, meditation serves to help one live with more compassion and understanding.

❋ And one more student shared that there is nothing scary about meditation, in fact it is the opposite of fear, it releases it. Meditation relaxes the practitioner and brings happiness and love. She shared that her experience with meditation is absolutely amazing because it allows her to connect with a source of energy that flows internally through her. She said she felt electrified after meditation.

Although the myths of meditation come in many images, from many traditions and cultures, and from many misconceptions, the most common myths about meditation involve chanting, twisted sitting position, strange hand gestures, and a quiet mind. These misconceptions have people believing that meditation is too difficult, it's only for others of different or Eastern cultures and requires too much money, time and energy to practice.

I am here to tell you that anyone can meditate.

Meditation is for anyone who wants to reduce their stress and bring more peace and harmony into their life. One great teacher said that if you are not able to meditate, then you have not learned how to harness the mind. To add to this I say that when you achieve intentional meditation, then you are beginning the process of managing the machine (the body, the mind, the emotions) rather than the machine managing you.

As an ex-corporate junkie in the pharmaceutical business, turned meditation practitioner and teacher of energy and spiritual practices, I can honestly say that meditation is beneficial to everyone. I can also say the when I meditate daily it keeps me from being that compulsive type A person. I have much more clarity because of meditation. There's a lot of gratitude within me because of my meditation practices and much more joy than I ever imagined possible.

While still working in corporate before I founded the Tree of Life Wellness Center in Huntington Beach, California, the presidents of these large pharmaceutical companies that I worked with asked me to teach them meditation. I found myself having sales meetings and they would start with a discussion about meditation and some basic techniques. The sales pitch became secondary. Meditation is for people in all types of business and business positions, not just those in pharmaceuticals and those that are presidents. It is also for urban housewives, the young, the old, the religious, the logical, the elderly and artists. The five Ws (who, what, where, when and why) and the how of meditation in the following chapter are tools for bringing prolonged awareness into your life more consciously and consistently, which is the foundation of meditation.

You will discover that the tools we share here will be beneficial in other parts of your life. For example, in the following chapters you will find that there's a tool to help you keep your cool when you are in traffic and it will help you get to your destination much more quickly. The tools are also useful to help you remain open to ongoing meditation and reveal the many treasures of meditation today and tomorrow.

2

MEDITATION: THREE WS AND HOW?

"Anyone who can think can meditate."

-Flower Newhouse

> *Where should I meditate?*
> *When is the best time to meditate?*
> *Do you need a teacher to meditate?*
> *What is the best position to successfully meditate?*
> *How you can start today?*

How many people in today's world have told you they have a quiet mind? Most people chatter on and on in their minds and never get any quiet time. The constant chatter consists of repetitive thoughts that is often circular and unproductive. Many meditation instructors, books and CDs prescribe meditation that occurs in complete stillness and quietness; however, these prescriptions are for people not running around with families, careers and a multitude of other responsibilities. I am here to remind you, there is no such thing as a quiet mind and total stillness. There is no such accomplishment in today's busy world as an empty mind and motionlessness. WOW! Isn't it a relief to know that there is no such thing as a quiet mind? Now, that you've made it this far we will assume you are willing to take the next steps away from the myths of meditation. You can allow meditation into your life by following these simple steps.

In order to have a good foundation for a lifelong meditation practice, let's begin with the positions that are not effective or necessary for meditation.

While lying on the floor or on a bed seems to be a comfortable meditation position, it's only going to get you relaxed enough to fall asleep, which is not meditating. Also, by lying on the floor or on a bed on your back, the energy that needs to flow throughout your body during meditation becomes stuck in your spine. Allowing energy to become stuck in your spine rather than letting it flow throughout your body is just another way to stress the body. The spine will get stiff and the muscles actually become energetically congested and tense. Moreover, meditating on your back for a prolonged period of time causes chronic back pain, which results in even greater stress and imbalance in the overall system, which defeats the purpose of meditation altogether.

Many books and CDs suggest that it is necessary to meditate sitting in the lotus posture, which is a cross-legged position sometimes used in yoga and advanced meditation. The fact is there is no need to sit lotus style. It is not a requirement to sit in positions that are so uncomfortable. Perhaps you already have experience with practicing yoga and meditation and the lotus position is comfortable for you. If that's the case, go ahead and sit in the lotus position. Most students cannot get into the proper lotus position in which the legs are crossed in such a way that each foot rests on top of the other leg's thigh and it looks like a pretzel. In addition, unless a student has been practicing yoga and sitting in the lotus position for extended periods of time, the lotus position is very uncomfortable. Rather than twisting your legs in an uncomfortable position, I encourage you to meditate in the seated position. Not only in a seated position, but use a chair for maximum comfort. Ideally a straight-backed chair.

Let me take you through some easy seated position steps that will allow you to meditate anywhere—well, almost anywhere, the airport is just too noisy and energetically congested to meditate effectively.

First, it's important to find a comfortable chair or sitting place to meditate in a seated position. Make sure you have enough space and are not too cramped. Some students complain that it's too difficult to meditate while in the seated position because the back begins to hurt. The back is not accustomed to much more than slouching. It took the muscles a while to get used to slouching and it may take a bit for the muscles to feel comfortable sitting with the spine as straight as possible. Although I have heard numerous times from students that their backs hurt when they try to meditate in a proper seated position (without leaning on the back of a chair), it is important to sit with a space between your back and the back of the chair. Our slouching, curved back habits result in most students wanting to sit and lean against the chair back, but leaning impedes the flow of energy. Ultimately the leaning on the chair back causes more stress and imbalance to the physical body as well as the energy body, which is the very thing meditation is meant to relieve.

Although in the beginning, many students feel discomfort in their spinal region when sitting with a straight back in the proper-seated position, the back and body begin to self adjust. Most of us spend our entire day, slouching, and the back complains by sending messages of ache and pain. This discomfort is only tempo-rary when your spine is straight and you are in the seated meditation posture because the back becomes increasingly more comfortable and relaxed. *See diagram on page 17.*

Take a moment and let's try the seated position posture. Sit in your chosen chair, straighten your spine, shoulders back, chin sightly lowered allowing the head to align on the shoulders so there's no tension or pressure. Feeling fantastic? It is likely that you will feel fantastic because the energy is flowing and the body is truly in alignment. Is your body telling you to slump because it is too uncomfortable to sit this way? Don't worry. The body rebels against the seated position because it has lost strength in the mid section, which has weakened the back muscles along the spine. It is important to tough this out and just go with it for a while. The best and ultimate way to sit while meditating is with a straight back/straight spine. Over time and put into practice, the proper seated position is more enjoyable because the muscles in your mid section and back increase in strength. You may even get a flat stomach if you practice this regularly enough.

Take another moment and think about how you are seated? Are you slouching? Is your head tilted back? If it is then the neck is going to ache. If you place your bum towards the edge of the chair, you will notice how the back self adjusts so that the spine is straight, without so much effort. It can be helpful to use a pillow or a wedge underneath your bum if sitting on the edge is too uncomfortable. Using a pillow or wedge is similar to using strengthened muscles. The pillow or wedge helps your spine to not tire so easily and thus you sit in a more aligned and proper meditation posture.

Believe it or not, the seated position is not only fundamental for meditation; it is also essential to improving all aspects of your life, which you'll learn about in later chapters.

Now that you are sitting with a straight back/straight spine, there are a few more basics to the seated position that are highly beneficial. Some books on meditation, have diagrams or photos that show meditation practitioners in seated positions holding their thumb and first finger closed or their thumb and second finger closed. Buddha himself is often shown with his hands clasped in different positions. These hand and finger positions are called *mudras*, which are any of the various positions in which the hands are held in Buddhist or Indian/Hindu yoga, meditation, dancing and even ritual practices. There is nothing wrong with using a mudra; however, unless the student is aware of the specifics, energy implications, and intentions of the mudra position, as well as the movement of energy as a result of the mudra, I recommend a different position for the hands and fingers.

While meditating in the seated position, leave your hands in an open and upward facing position. Keep your palms facing upward toward the sky and all fingers open and receptive. This is the most receptive position for your hands and fingers and allows your body to release any excess energy that you might accumulate during meditation. Keeping your palms open allows your energy channels to be open and the flow of energy in and out is without break or obstacle when there is no mudra or closed finger position.

Next, it is ideal to place the tip of your tongue on the roof of your mouth during meditation. Remember when you were a child and you curled your tongue backwards—this is the position you want to use. Placing the tip of your tongue on the roof of your mouth allows energy to balance the left brain and the right brain, as well as the left and right body. Although most students think that their tongue is naturally in this position, this is not the natural resting position of the tongue. Allowing the tongue to rest on the roof of your mouth all day, every day allows you to be more connected to all things and to everything. It also allows your brain and body to function more effectively as a whole. Placing the tip of your tongue on the roof of your mouth creates an energy channel, called the central meridian. It is a pathway in the body which the energy of the body is believed to flow. It is complete and connected.

There is one side effect to placing the tip of your tongue on the roof of your mouth—the sensation that you are going to yawn. This is a natural reaction. To yawn is to take in a long,deep breath. The tongue connection technique creates the sensation of a yawn because the position allows more oxygen into your system as if through a yawn—a long deep breath. Breathing **without** the tongue connected to the roof of the mouth is like getting one-fourth of the lung capacity for air. Placing the tip of the tongue on the roof of the mouth actually allows the body to rest. To breathe in and out through the nostrils allows the lungs to expand more fully and receive more oxygen.

There are other benefits in placing the tip of your tongue on the roof of your mouth which are experienced everyday. Try the tongue connection technique while driving. It allows you to get to your destination quicker. Really, I'm not kidding. Try it and experience the ease in which you move through traffic. Having the tip of the tongue connected to the roof of the mouth actually allows for greater capacity of oxygen into the lungs and body systems.

The reasons for using a seated position with a straight back/ straight spine, keeping your palms facing upward and open with fingers in a receptive position, and placing the tip of your tongue on the roof of your mouth during meditation or daily activities is twofold.

1. **A prolonged awareness.** Achieving prolonged awareness helps the mind to have a break from the daily tasks and mind chatter. Prolonged awareness recharges the mind. Therefore, it is something you want in life. With the practice of meditation, prolonged awareness will develop and grow. It is as if your mind has experienced repeated naps that refresh and rejuvenate the mind, the organs and the body.

2. **The down pouring of energy.** When meditating in a seated position with hands in an open and upward (palms facing the

ceiling) position, and with the tongue connection technique the brain is more easily recharged with energy that comes into the top of your head.

This is the energetic place (the energy from the top of your head or your crown chakra) that plugs you into source, spirit, God, the creator, or whatever it is you call this origin of energy current. It is a goal to allow this energy into your body so that you reap the most benefits from your meditation and this particular seated position is key. *See below.*

When new fresh energy pours into your crown then you have more peace and longer periods of internal calm. As the new energy pours in, then the pineal gland activates and there is access to higher wisdom, access to more intelligence and ease with problem solving.

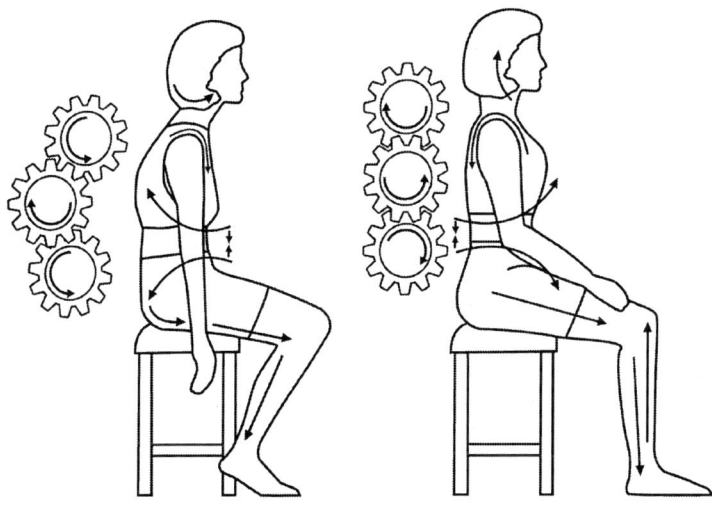

Correct vs. Incorrect Posture

3

THE TIME TO MEDITATE: LOOKING FORWARD TO MEDITATION

*All meditation must begin with arousing
deep compassion. Whatever one does must
emerge from an attitude of love and of
benefiting others.*

-Milarepa

> *I have to meditate when it's completely quiet - everywhere.*
> *What is the best time to meditate?*
> *I can't find the time to meditate, what should I do?*

Recently I had dinner with a friend of mine while I was out of town. We had dinner on a Tuesday night, which is the night that I meditate at our center with my advanced meditation students. The Tuesday meditation group has met consistently for more than seven years. During dinner, my friend told me he felt as if his energy was expanding on his crown and he said it felt like pressure (the top of the head responsible for one of the major energy centers). I smiled and told him that my soul was called to meditate with my students and my crown chakra automatically activated as if I was there with them. This can happen more automatically to you if you are consistent with your practice.

Once you have started meditating at the same time and the same place, your soul develops what I call a meditation alarm clock. Your soul, your physical body, and your energy body get nourishment from meditating. Once you practice consistently at a similar time and place, then the soul and energy body want to be fed by the sustenance of meditation and will prepare as if that is about to occur. During this time, it is easier to connect and more will flow in your meditation.

A student of mine that facilitates the Monday night meditation at the center has had a similar experience. Every Monday evening, regardless of where she is or what she is doing, she is "called", so to speak, to our center. She, too, has developed an inner alarm clock that sounds to tell her that it is time to meditate.

The soul, once activated to meditate, wants to continue and will create opportunities for the human to encounter these opportunities. Whether through a teacher, a center, group, meditating while in nature or whatever the mechanism, the soul, once attuned to the universal light energy, will seek it out.

Even though meditating at a consistent time and place seems rigid, the point of meditation in today's environment is **not** about adhering to steadfast rules. The point is to reap the benefits of meditation, which include mental, emotional and physical well-being. There are also, if you can take that leap, spiritual and higher creative benefits. According to most books and many teachers, the best time to meditate is in the morning. Most literature suggests morning meditation so you start your day off with a calm perspective, clearer insight, and inner reflection. Although meditation first thing in the morning is highly beneficial, if you are like me, then the best time of day is **not** in the morning. When I wake, it seems that my mind has been turned on super high speed and is set to rapid fire - going through what I need to take care of for the day. So, I decided that I needed to find another time that worked for my busy mind. When I had a dog to walk every morning, it was great. It would give me the needed space, which allowed my mind to wind down, and reflect on what I did the day before that needed to be improved upon. Having spent many years in the corporate world with my corporate head quarters often located on the east coast, I got into a routine of meditating around 3 p.m. Now I have a different routine and I have discovered that the best time of day for me to meditate is when I have most of my "gotta take care of this immediately list completed". For me, meditation now often happens to be in the morning.

The best time to meditate is not the same for everyone. Many of my students that have varying schedules and personalities have shared that meditation works best: after work, after working out, before the kids wake up and even in the middle of the night. You will need to identify your ideal time to meditate. The key is consistent practice.

When identifying the ideal time and place to mediate, consider the following:

1. **Meditate after a shower.** Meditation is easier after a shower. If you want to meditate after work, then it is best to take a shower beforehand to remove the energies of others that you have picked up during the day.

2. **Meditate after removing your shoes.** It is ideal to remove your shoes before meditation. Your shoes pick up energy from every place that you step once you are outside. Think of the Asian tradition of taking your shoes off before entering the home. Leaving the outside energy that you have on your shoes

out of your meditation is great because you then are not bothered by anyone else's energy but yours. Even if you are meditating at work doing some of our "Two Minute Meditations," taking your shoes off for this brief interval will have a much more restorative experience.

3. **Meditate after working out.** Meditation after working out is good because you have just released old energies that have been stuck in and around your body. One of the very reasons meditation can be challenging is because you have so many thoughts racing through your mind that are specific to old issues, worries, frustrations, resentments, and energies held in by the cells of our bodies. By working out, you release enough of these old issues and energies so meditation comes much easier. (OK, yes, and your mind will be a lot more quiet,). You will also have a deeper meditation experience.

4. **Recommended pre and post meditation exercises.** These exercises take only a few minutes and make meditation a truly wonderful experience. Many people think that it is best to just sit and meditate. This is true, using simple exercises designed to release the old energy, can help the mind become clear, and creates the opportunity for meditation to be deeper and quieter. Even after 15 years of daily meditation, I need to do some very basic exercises. I find that when I don't it takes longer to get into a quiet place and fully enjoy the experience. *Skip to Page 38 for these exercises.*

5. **Eating moderately or lightly before meditating.** I recall going to a retreat center and being told that I was not allowed to eat or drink anything until 1 p.m. First, I was mortified and thought how impossible this would be. After thinking a little more, I laughed and promptly made sure that I packed enough food to nosh on for breakfast so that I wouldn't be meditating on how loud my stomach moaned. I have discovered that meditating on an empty stomach, though many of the sages and

teachers say an empty stomach is best, means that I am meditating on when and what I am going to eat. So, it is best not to
meditate on an empty stomach. On the other hand, if you have
eaten too much before meditation you will be meditating on
why you ate so much. So, don't meditate on a full stomach
either.

6. **Removing a watch and all jewelry prior to meditation.** Do
   not wear a watch or jewelry during meditation. Watches and
   jewelry collect energy from daily life. If you wear something
   daily then all good and not so good energies are collected and
   can be brought into your meditation. Jewelry emits energy into
   the space in which you are meditating and can contribute to a
   busy mind. Give yourself a rest from the old energies that are
   carried in your watch and jewelry. Ideally, you want to free
   yourself from these things so that your body rests from the con-
   fines of the stuff that you carry.

7. **Meditation before bed is very bothersome to your elec-
   trical system and not recommended.** Surprisingly, meditation actually energizes your brain and system. If you are considering meditation before bed, I recommend that you meditate at
   least an hour before you get in bed to sleep. If you try meditation before bed and it works for you, great, then that is when
   you need to meditate.

8. **Listening to a meditation CD while behind the wheel.** You
   may laugh, but in every class I have taught someone always asks
   about meditation CD's: "Can you meditate while driving?"
   Meditation while driving is **not** ideal. You are already in a type
   of mesmerized state while driving because of the lines on the
   road. It's also not a good idea to close your eyes while driving.
   What you can do is put your tongue on the roof of your mouth.
   It will help to get your brain and body balanced and more
   aligned to being calm, and help get to your destination quicker.

Every class I dare the students to try this one just to see if it works.

9. **Any time you are feeling angry only helps you to meditate on the anger.** Although it may seem like a good idea to meditate if you are feeling angry or after you have just had an argument, it is **not** a good idea. Meditating after an argument only magnifies the energy and issue at the cause of your anger.

10. **Meditation while you are feeling fidgety is actually good.** If you find yourself fidgeting during meditation practice and you stay in meditation, know this is a good sign and that you are doing a great job. If you are moving violently then this is not a good thing and it is best to stop meditating.

If you don't chose the ideal time to meditate, then you'll find excuses not to meditate. You will discover that your brain will take the time to engage in prolonged awareness in some other way and the monkey mind and the negative thoughts begin to take over. Consider the ideal time to meditate as your personal time (just minutes a day) and that it is as important as brushing your teeth and more important than your morning coffee. Remember, it brings the benefits of healing, restoration, happiness and allows more fun.

Meditation is just as important as brushing your teeth

Once you have found the ideal time to meditate then you'll want to identify a specific place to meditate. Meditation is that much more effective when you have found your ideal place to because you've prepared your mind and space and set the tone/energy which allows your meditation to be easier. If you cannot seem to find an ideal place to consistently meditate consider these options:

1. In a chair. Meditation in a seated position is best because it increases the awareness of the brain and the body. Again, many people believe that meditating in bed is effective; however, I say leave the bed for sleeping. Your brain and your body have been trained to know that sleeping takes place while lying in bed. Meditating in a seated position is ideal.

2. A place your pet hangs out. A simple way to find an ideal place to meditate is to notice the place your pet hangs out. Pets seem to know the best energetic places in your home.

3. In a closet. Meditation in a closet is not an ideal place to meditate, but if you have children at home, it may be difficult to find the time and place to meditate. One of my students said the closet was the best place for her to meditate. Using headphones, she meditated to a guided practice and had much more calm and sanity to deal with the chaos of her family.

4. A special pillow. A pillow is a useful tool for creating an ideal place to meditate because you can carry it around with you and make it personally yours. You can also use a pillow cover or piece of cloth in the same way that you would use a pillow. To make meditation energetically consistent, using a pillow, pillow cover or cloth is helpful in allowing the energy to be drawn to a consistent space. When I was in my corporate jobs I carried a pillow cover with me, which helped me to create an ideal place for meditation while I was traveling or in the office.

5. A yoga mat. A yoga mat can be a useful tool for meditation; however, only use a yoga mat that you will use specifically for meditating. Using a mat that is used for yoga in a studio carries energy from the floor similar to the energy that your shoes carry—it is not always the cleanest or clearest energy.

6. A place in nature. A garden, a beach, park or any place outdoors can be an ideal place to meditate. These places in nature give rise to natural elements such as the sound of wind, waves birds. Just listening can be a form of meditation. What is the wind, the

water or the bird saying? Meditate on the sounds of nature as a way to develop prolonged awareness. But don't meditate in direct sun unless it is only for a few minutes. The sun's energy is too intense and can create more stress in the long run.

7. A church or monastery. A church or a monastery can be an ideal place to meditate because it is a place that has icons or images of saints and holy teachers. Keeping your awareness on an icon or image of a saint or holy one keeps you in contact with the higher energy of the creative power. Regardless of your religion, you can utilize the images of spiritual teachers, or spaces to meditate.

8. A teacher-guided meditation. Having a guru to meditate with is not necessary, but having a guide or a teacher in the beginning is helpful. People who have been trained in various forms of meditation have an insight into what works and does not work, and what pitfalls you may have during meditation practice. Meditation is good for you, but like all things, with moderation. A teacher can help ensure that you are regulating your practice and that you are not over-energizing your system. If you meditate a lot, you can activate and over energize your energy body, which can cause what has been termed Kundalini Syndrome (for more information about Kundalini Syndrome go to http://www.SheevaunMoran.com/blog).

9. A group Meditation. Meditating with a class or a group of people is not necessary. However, meditating in a group can help you stay committed to a regular time and place of meditation practice. Meditation with a group also helps to magnify the down-pouring of energy for you and for others. Group meditation is often practiced to help heal the earth. You've probably heard of groups praying for an area to be healed of violence, well this is how meditation works in groups. It allows positive energies to magnify in intensity by hundreds. Meditating with a group magnifies the energy, experience and result.

Meditation is a great healing and a centering tool. Consistent meditation practice can eventually allow you to meditate any time and any place. Once you have been consistent with meditation you can bring it into every moment of your life and you will find that you are in a more ease filled space no matter what is going on around you.

It is important that you identify the ideal time and place to meditate. Again, one reason for this is continuity, but more importantly meditating at the same time daily or weekly in a place that is ideal makes meditation easier by accessing energy that is set for you. Meditating regularly creates an opportunity for instant meditation. It also accumulates or draws more energy to a specific place and infuses that space with more peace and healing. Do your best to be consistent with the time and place that you meditate. If you have decided to meditate on Monday's then stick to that day. The reason for this is, again, is that your body is more receptive to the down-pouring of new and fresh energy.

Obviously this list sounds like a lot of do's and don'ts, but if you are finding that you are getting serious about meditation these are very useful suggestions to help you have the best meditation experience.

Your objective is to find a time and place that works for you and use that until you are ready for the next step.

Meditation is meant to be restorative.

While it can seem like a chore at times, it is still worth the effort over the long haul. Your physical, mental and emotional energy body accumulates data every time you meditate. As you meditate, those energies that you access and those accumulated experiences, even if you don't recall them, are part of your overall energy map. It's as if you are doing a reset and upload each time you meditate. The fragments of life are the sum of your energy body and the energy body is like a windshield. The more mud you have on the windshield, the more you need to cleanse it. That's why a reset is beneficial because the reset is just like starting fresh.

Once you've have had a wonderful, expansive experience meditating, you usually desire to have the exact same experience again. Too often people give up once they've had an extraordinary experience because they do not have that same blissful experience in the following sessions. This is not the time to give up. It just means that there's another level you need to achieve in order to get to that expansive place or feeling once again. It is said that if you have a few of those over a year's time then you are fortunate.

It is common that most people may only experience blackness in their meditation. Experiencing blackness is fine. It is good. It is just one level of the meditation experience. Regardless of the level of meditation experience, most people who meditate will experience peace and an overall calmer life, less anxiety, better sleep, happier relationships. Just because you are not experiencing some fantastical feeling or phenomena during meditation doesn't mean that you are not getting the benefits of the meditation session. The experiences of meditation practice are often cumulative. It's worth it to continue because your body and soul records every ounce of meditation and the experiences that accompany meditation practice.

Perseverance and consistency are the keys. Just because you aren't completely emptying your mind or just because you feel uncomfortable doesn't mean that you aren't having success. Our physical, emotional, mental and energy bodies crave inner calm, but you'll need to learn how to bring some of that inner calm to all aspects of your life through meditation. Similar to when you learned how to ride a bike, there are bumps along the way. Finding the time and place to meditate consistently are just tiny pebbles in your shoe.

My personal reason for continuing to meditate daily is simply because I feel as happy inside as I am outside when I'm done with my meditation. So, I am actually as happy as I think I am just through daily meditation practice. That feeling of happiness became something that I want to feel every day and is what has kept me meditating daily. Over the past 15 years I have seldom missed meditating daily. If I did miss meditating, I felt as if the world was crazy and I was going along with the craziness. Meditation continues to give me the insight to be creative, happier, have more energy, ease with problem solving and the ability to be a compassionate being with ease. For me, it's about being happier no matter what happens! So, today and every day, I look forward to meditation.

4

EXERCISE AND MEDITATION

In order to become more spiritual,
you have to acknowledge the physical.

-Sheevaun Moran

Meditation is just sitting there?
What has exercise got to do with it?

You may be wondering what exercise has to do with meditation. Many of my students have said that on the first day of class. Often people show up with yoga mats and blankets. When I talk about the body and how to achieve the ultimate peace and calm when meditating, I go into the benefits of exercise. The look on their faces when I ask them to start exercises is priceless. It's both a sense of shock and denial. But simply put, it is **not** natural for the body to be sedentary. Why not incorporate a few, only a few, minutes of extremely simple exercises in order to get the most out of meditation and feel healthier. Just know that these exercises are so simple that an 80 year old can do them.

Now that you have discovered the ideal time and place to meditate, the physical body needs to be prepared too. The purpose for these basic exercises is to prepare the body for the inflow and down pouring of new energy. When one is meditating, the purpose is often to achieve a calm state of being, improved health, or connection to a higher self. But the overall effect of meditation is allowing new energy to enter your system, your body, your aura. It's new energy that allows the mind and body to eliminate the old to restore and refresh. The use of simple exercises, gives you the ability to meditate easier, remain in meditation longer and receive new energy with fewer obstacles.

When you meditate, you are displacing the old energy with new. The objective is to invigorate the body/system. Remember the saying "Do not put new wine into an old wine bag". This applies to meditation. By using simple exercises, you gain the space within the system to allow new energy to penetrate the body, mind, and cells.

Many people feel like they are going to sleep while meditating. They can't remember anything. Essentially, what has happened is that the down pouring of new energy has overwhelmed the body and circuits. The body is overwhelmed, and it seems as if the body is sleeping. But it is really taking a break (a time out) and regulating the energy receptacle, the body. So if you've ever come out of meditation feeling really tired, as if you haven't received anything from the session, it's an indicator that your body needs to release old energy. In other words move about or get active. The exercise routine allows the body's circuits to prepare for new energy pouring in. The new energy is necessary for the body to restore itself. If you think of someone who is calmer, you may notice the person looks younger. The same applies to people who meditate; they are restoring their system and appear more youthful and energetic. The new energy brought in through meditation helps to regenerate and activate the connection to your body-self, wisdom-self, and divine-self. I've had husbands call call me to say thanks because their wives are much more vibrant and youthful since they started meditating. Wives have called me to say that since their husbands have begun meditation, there is a sense of peace and clarity within their family.

Having done yoga for most of my life, it is important to note that these specific exercises, in the following pages, help to release toxins, energies and blockages in the major energy centers and organs of the body. These mini exercises are done in a sequence so toxins move are easily release. Not only are they good to do prior to meditation, these exercises are also good for overall health and improvement of the body. These exercises help to activate all of the chakras in the body. Chakras that work properly provide additional energy to the body and circuits of each system (endocrine system, nervous system, and skeletal system).

"What is in motion stays in motion". ~ Albert Einstein

The Lymphatic system is responsible for every ounce of our blood. It transports fats and proteins, while filering debris from the tissues. When the body gets exercise, our lymphatic system starts to work properly. These exercises release toxins from our blood. They enable our organs to activate and clear stagnation. Exercise helps to flush out the old junk left from years of accumulated worry, fear, anxiety, tension, stress, resentment, and bad food.

How often do you get up and move during the day? I would bet not much. People who have office jobs are sitting in front of a computer all day long, in the same position. When you are hunched in the same position for a prolonged period, you create a blockage within the free movement of your spinal energy and spinal fluid. Soon it becomes habit for the muscles resulting in negative stress and tension. Ultimately, there is constriction in the lungs which restricts the restoration and ease of the body to breathe regularly. Just by hunching over for a long period of time, you restrict the diaphragm from allowing the lungs to fully inflate. Bodies that are sedentary have more artery calcification. This can lead to arthritis, frozen shoulder, spinal issues, muscular strain, headaches and other maladies.

Exercise can help activate a stagnant colon, which can often relieve irritable bowl syndrome. Endorphins get released which tends to make people happier.

When I began teaching meditation, my regular gym routine quickly went by the wayside. I was teaching a great number of meditation classes and found that my body was in better shape than it had ever been. I never really thought about this while it was happening, until someone commented on how much I must exercise to be in such good shape. Why was I in such good shape? I was doing mini-exercises four times a day. I had greater endurance and strength. I often tell the story of how for years I wanted to have better abs. It didn't matter how many sit-ups I did, there was no significant improvement. But when I began these mini-exercises, along with using the breathing exercises (See chapter 6), my abs suddenly became stronger and more defined. Of course no one will ever say I have abs of steel, but my inner core is much stronger. Over the years, many of my students have shared similar success stories. There have been stories about losing weight, eating better and having a more positive attitude from exercise and basic meditation. One even shared that her osteoporosis disappeared!

A man in one of my classes, who was overweight and very quiet, attended each of my five sessions of basic meditation. After four weeks of consistently coming to class, I noticed something different about him. On the last day of class, I asked him what he got out of the sessions. He explained that he had been an Orange County Transit Authority (OCTA) bus driver for more than 20 years. Since he began exercise and meditation, he was happier. He had also quit drinking with his buddies after work, lost 35 pounds and had started exercising daily. Everyone in the class, me included, was stunned. Wow! An incredible transformation had happened in such a short amount of time.

Again, exercise before meditation helps the body receive the down-pouring of new energy that occurs during meditation. It is important to do these exercises (listed below) to receive maximum benefit from your meditation practice. Obviously, if you already have an exercise routine you can incorporate some of these to achieve more balance.

1. Eyes rolls. Roll your eyes around in a big circle around the room to the right 12 times. If you have trouble rolling your eyes, use your finger to create a big circle and follow your finger with your eyes. Or just look up, then right, then left, then down. Then roll your eyes to the left 12 times.

2. Head turns. Turn your head on your shoulders to the right and then to the left. Do this 12 times.

3. Head tilt. Tilt your head forward (chin to chest) and back (head backward with eyes to the sky) 12 times. Do this gently. Your neck is not accustomed to this much movement. There may be cracking, but this is just energy being released.

4. Shoulder shrug. Shrug your shoulders up and tense your body as tightly as possible, even tensing your facial muscles. Inhale for a count of two. Let go of all the tension. Exhale three times. (doing this at the end of a particularly stressful day will ease a tremendous amount of tension you've stored in your body).

5. Shoulder roll. Roll your shoulders backward in a circle like motion 12 times. Next, roll your shoulders forward in a circle like motion 12 times.

6. Spine/Arm rotation. Keeping your hips stationary, raise your arms with your elbows bent to shoulder height, your palms facing outward and twist from right to left 12 times. The key to this exercise is to keep your hips still. If you have a bad back,

start slowly. This exercise actually releases kinks in your back and strengthens your spine and back muscles.

7. Hula. With your feet shoulder width apart, rotate your hips as if doing a hula dance or swinging a hoop to the right 12 times. Then go to the left 12 times. I call this doing a little bit of Elvis.

8. Knee rotations. Place the palms of your hands over your kneecaps grasping them lightly. Slowly and gently rotate your knees to the right 12 times, then rotate your knees to the left 12 times.

9. Squats. In a comfortable stance with your feet shoulder width apart, bounce gently bending your knees over your toes. Do this 50 times.

10. Foot rotations. Raise your right leg slightly from the ground so your foot is in the air. Hold on to something if needed for balance. Rotate your right foot to the right 12 times then rotate your right foot to the left 12 times. Next, raise your left leg so your foot is slightly off the ground. Rotate your left foot to the right 12 times, then to the left 12 times.

11. Toe point. Raise your right leg so your foot is off the ground. Point your toes upward toward the sky, then downward toward the ground. Do this 12 times. Switch to your left foot. Point your toes toward the sky, then downward to the ground. Again, do this 12 times.

12. Shoulder stress release. Place the palms of your hands on your shoulders. Grab all of the stress energy from your shoulders and throw it vigorously into the ground.

NOTE: Do this sequence 12 times each.
To watch a live demonstration of these exercises go to http://LearnToMeditateIn2Minutes.com/book-videos.html

Remember the windshield metaphor. Just as we want to keep the windshield of our car cleansed from the dust and dirt that mud-dies our vision while driving, we want to keep our body systems cleansed and free from energetic mud that blocks, pollutes and contaminates the energy and bodily systems. Exercise is the first form of cleansing the windshield of our systems. As the first form of cleansing, exercise helps to prepare the body systems for the down-pouring of new energy that is received during meditation. These mini exercises only take a few minutes; and the overall health benefits are cumulative over time.

5

THE BENEFITS OF MEDITATION: PHYSICAL, MENTAL, EMOTIONAL AND SPIRITUAL

"One has to try to develop one's inner feelings, which can be done simply by training one's mind. This is a priceless human asset and one you don't have to pay income tax on!"

-His Holiness Dalai Lama

So, what is this trend that says meditation is beneficial to health?
Is meditation just like yoga waiting to get popular?
Has meditation been around for a long time?
Do people that meditate really understand the benefits?

The point of a two-minute meditation is about reaping the benefits of what meditation does for you physically, mentally, emotionally and spiritually as quickly as possible. I'm here to help you - truly learn for the first time how to practice meditation and find peace and health in your otherwise hectic life. All the techniques within this book derive from my own personal experience, first as a practitioner then as a teacher of meditation. The techniques shared here are from years of my own frustration of not being able to get peaceful health in my body, mind and life. This is the essences of many masters, living teachers, teachers who have passed on, and a plethora of books. The techniques do not come from or contradict any religion, guru or other practice you are involved with and will only enhance your life in many ways.

These meditation techniques are simple and yet special in the way they work.

Over the past several years, the cover of almost every health magazine promotes meditation and yoga as a way to achieve health and peace. Each year at least one major magazine has gone so far as to show different perspectives on God. Even the quintessential magazine *Time* has featured God on its cover and in its pages. Major publications are also showing how traditional western medicine is beginning to embrace alternatives to physical, mental, emotional, and spiritual health. One magazine presented documented studies telling us how well-respected physicians at major teaching universities (Harvard, Cornell, Oxford) are bringing meditation and energy healing to their patients. Physicians are regularly recommending meditation to their patients as a way to combat stress. Hospitals are hosting free energy healing and meditation classes for their community. Universities are offering courses for certification in yoga, health, and meditation. Corporations have invited me in to help their staff achieve greater peace, which results in greater productivity, less negativity, higher profitability and happier, solution-oriented employees.

The meditation trend is no longer a trend it is a way of life.

We live in a society of the quick fix, a society where everything can be fixed by taking a pill. For some, meditation may seem like taking a step backward. As we get into the issues surrounding meditation, you will find that it will actually take you forward to creative places and new solutions. You will move forward with ease and better overall health. Not only will meditation get you moving forward, it will have a ripple effect and create a friendlier environment. It will access your soul spot, keep you grounded and present in every action.

Through meditation, you will achieve a better family life and upbeat work environment. Through meditation anger is released and that those frequent bouts of depression, frustration and hopelessness, diminish. Meditation is not a one-time fix; it is a free prescription for a life.

Physical Benefits:
Improved health and a tool for healing the body. You may have heard that meditation can help the body. This is true. Meditation can change the physiology of your body allowing it to heal itself. Most of our bodies have become accustomed to the fight or flight mode that comes from the stress of daily living. This constant negative stress that fight or flight puts on the body helps accelerate the break down of the cells, muscles and tissues and results in the feeling of constant fatigue. The chemical structure of the brain changes from breaking down to restorative when one meditates. It allows the brain and body to heal itself. The greatest healing occurs during sleep, which is why you will feel the need to sleep more if

you've been sick or have used up your reserves. Two Minute Meditations act like a power nap. Longer meditations can be like an entire night of sleep.

Students in my meditation classes have shared stories of illnesses which have disappeared because they are meditating regularly. Meditation reduces the negative stress that takes a toll on our physical bodies. If you know how to transmute that negative energy into positive energy through specific advanced meditations, then you will have a stronger physical, mental and emotional body. It wasn't until my body had become very sick from a stress-induced condition, that I incorporated meditation into my daily routine. The results was good health. Our bodies become acidic from the stress of over-stimulation and the many responsibilities we have. Meditation helps realign the imbalance in the chemical structure to a more neutral place, so we are refreshed and energized. This is a more natural state of well being.

The physical body, similar to the brain, needs rest. Meditation gives the physical body the rest it needs while in an awaken state. It allows the mind time to process and discard what is not necessary. If both the body and mind are under constant duress, eventually there is a malfunction. Meditation in Two Minutes helps the body restore and alleviates the burden if used in regular intervals (say 3-5 times per day). Duress in the body produces highly toxic chemicals that the body must break down and eliminate. Meditation helps to reduce the duress and the toxic chemicals. Meditation gives your body an inner calm that affects your mental and emotional health as well. Meditation increases your lung capacity, which can increase your body's ability to purify toxins and provide more energy. Meditation strengthens your back muscles and your spine. It also strengthens the muscles around your head, neck, and face. When you are injured, the body becomes more efficient at healing when practicing meditation regularly. Meditation changes the way your physical body vibrates with energy. You vibrate at higher energy levels when you practice meditation regularly. You can achieve more in the same amount of time through the benefits of meditation. Your focus and attention becomes more effective when you meditate regularly.

Mental Benefits:
The mind has more clarity, ease and calm. Our minds are crowded with thoughts and constant chatter of life's how, why and when, we are constantly challenged by our hectic lifestyles and schedules. Meditation gives the brain a rest from the intensity (or should I say insanity) of our repetitive thoughts and responsibilities. Meditation is our opportunity to hear quiet. We have forgotten what it is like to hear quiet because we have become so conditioned to add noise. Quiet has become something to fill. Our minds become more proficient at processing life's information once it is properly and regularly rested.

Meditation is our opportunity to hear quiet.

Better business. I discovered that meditation helped me clear my mind and respond faster. I could soon close business deals faster. It became easier to communicate in difficult situations. I had more free time to go after new deals. Company profits rose. More on page 46.

More positive thoughts and sense of well being. Negative thoughts often irritate or agitate us into a state of stress, anger, frustration and cloudy thinking. Meditation helps to change our negative thoughts. By simply breathing and meditating on uplifting thoughts or words, you can affect positive change in yourself and our environment. Creativity and the freedom to be more creative is a benefit. Controlling thoughts that control you are eliminated through meditation. Negative thinking is often repetitive and leaves us without resolution. Some call it circling the drain.

Because of meditation or inner reflection we become the managers of the mind and thoughts rather than our thoughts controlling or managing our mind and actions.

Forgiveness. One of the exercises that I share in my meditation classes is forgiveness. Because we are often stuck in the same thinking patterns of who did what to whom and how much it hurt we create cloudy thinking patterns. Meditation can release the patterns of holding grudges and allow forgiveness.

Emotional Benefits:

A feeling of peace. I had a student who was a plumber and was on the road a lot. His wife had sent him to my class to learn to meditate because he used to come home raging or telling stories about how he raged at others throughout his day. He told me a story about how meditation helped him one day when he was stuck in traffic and someone cut him off. His past tendency was to use a lot of sign language and yell. When he was being harassed by the other driver, he said that he easily let the guy have the spot in front of him. Then a weird thing happened. The guy who cut him off abruptly stopped, got out of his car and came back and screamed and then proceeded to break the plumber's truck side mirror. The plumber said that he was so calm about the whole thing, considering that in the past he would have gotten out of the truck and begun to fist fight. He said that each of his interactions throughout his day were no longer filled with rage and anger but peace and acceptance. Many other students have told me they were having anger issues until they started meditating regularly. They began to feel a sense of peace, not anger.

A healthier sense of self. I remember the first time my mind was actually quiet. Because of that one experience and recollection, I am able to be quiet more often. Because of that one experience, I can connect to it any time and have a much more peaceful meditation or moment. That first time of quiet was attained through participating in a particular meditation (Twin Hearts). When I woke up the next day, I felt like I had found my true happy self and I was hooked on meditating regularly. This is what I wish for you, because once you feel it, you will feel like you know what you are supposed to feel and yet have not yet accessed.

Recently a student was talking about their issues throughout the week. Their conversation was all over the map with incomplete sentences, thoughts that were bouncing from one subject to the next in rapid succession, and it was too difficult to follow anything they were talking about. He told me he was tired, overwhelmed and had just yelled at a vendor. "So when was the last time you meditated?", I asked. He sat there for several minutes and just continued to blame this person and blame that event. Then he sat back, took a breath, and finally heard the question about when he'd last meditated and realized that each scenario was solvable had he taken the time to meditate.

My students have shared many stories regarding a sense of self they had never felt before because of the simplicity of these techniques. Had they learned some of these coping techniques earlier in life, they would have been much more peaceful and fulfilled. *Let's share these with our children so they don't have the same challenges when they get into school or business.*

Capture precious time – or rather expand the time that you already have. Not only did I feel more at ease from meditation, I also found that I had more time. It seemed like the more I practiced meditation, the more I was able to accomplish in less time. I always had the ability to do a lot but as time marched on with more and more stressors, time seemed elusive. When I started to meditate, regularly, I found that I had more time for myself.

Ability to let go. We have the tendency to hold on to what is no longer necessary in our lives and through meditation we can let go. Because we have been taught that the past is important somehow that has translated into believing that we need to hang

on to the past when it's only important to recall it. There is no need
to live there and hold on. Letting go is just as much a learned
behavior as holding on. We don't come into life with the ability to
hold on. Through meditation, we can live in the here and now and
"just be".

Just because the phrase "letting go" may concern, don't think
you have to let go of everything. It's a process and one that will
happen gradually. Your old negative emotions will be loosened and
you'll be much happier. Things that you didn't even recall that you
needed to release can be let go. You don't even need to be conscious about what you are going to let go of, all you need to do is
allow the space and time to meditate and it naturally occurs on its
own. Remember that letting go is a good thing and leads to many
rewards.

Business Benefits:
Less Stress. I came from a corporate way of life where stress
was part of the job. Meditation brings about a better way of being,
particularly in the business world.

*Your entire way of being in business is more grounded and
real when you meditate.*

Through regular meditation, your body will become more
vibrant, You will attract more business and may even eliminate the
need for another cup of $4 coffee. You can actually use the breath
techniques in the following chapter to calm an entire room down. I
used to use this technique when the room was noisy and everyone
seemed to want to talk at the same time.

The go-go-go lifestyle of business often make you a Type-A
personality and you can soon become overwhelmed. Meditation

will help you focus on one item at a time, even though you've been trained to think that multi-tasking is the best way to get things done. It's really "one tasking" that is going help you through life and meditation gives you that ability.

More productive. You'll be much more productive just by using the simple techniques from these pages. You won't need to force yourself to do more, clarity and productivity will increase exponentially because of meditation.

Creativity increases. Because your brain and body will be clearer through meditation, your creativity will soar. When there's too much going on and the negative stress is taking its toll, that's when creativity is challenged.

Problem solving is more effortless. The issues which often seemed to hold you back begin to dissolve. Situations that seemed to take a long time to solve become easily resolved. Your mind is clear, your energy is fluid and your problem-solving capabilities become effortless. Your decision making will improve after meditating for a while. Situations will seem to resolve without so much of you time and energy.

Ability to handle multiple situations with ease. Just as a car cannot function without an oil change, meditation helps our ability to handle multiple issues with ease. Think of coming back from vacation and being able to handle just about any number of issues, and then that begins to wear off. Daily meditation is your mini-vacation so that you're able to handle multiple situations each and every day.

More prosperous. One thing that meditation results in is manifestation. Once we meditate regularly, we stop wishing and start manifesting.

Spiritual Benefits:
New ways of living and connecting more deeply. Although we're not going to delve into the spiritual side of meditation in this

book, just know that whatever religion you practice you will become more connected to your own spirituality through a simple process. Techniques have been designed to give anyone at any age or religious background, the ability to practice without interfering with their own belifs. I have students from all walks of religion and life, that tell me they continue to use these techniques and incorporate them into their spiritual practice. It has helped them more deeply embrace their own religious practices.

Regardless of where you are in your spiritual evolution to have reminders or new ways of thinking is always beneficial.

We can experience new people, more open attitudes and different cultures through meditation.

Overall Benefits:
More relaxed, happy, healthy, vibrant, content, ease, grace and positive.

When people talk to me about meditation, they often slip up and say "medication". So in reality, meditation can actually become like a medication. If taken daily, the benefits far outweigh the challenges and it's one of the few things that are free. You will likely sleep better just by doing these techniques. Many people have gotten off their prescriptions just by incorporating meditation.

Don't let the opportunity to learn to meditate pass you by. You may be passing up the chance to reward yourself with good health, happiness and interaction with wonderful people. Remember that like attracts like and it's easier when you meditate to attract healthier, happier and more vibrant people into your life.

When you practice meditation often and properly every facet of your life improves.

It takes 21 days to eliminate an old habit and the same 21 days to incorporate a new habit. Try these techniques for 21 days and see what miracles occur in your life.

6

In the Air: Breathing the Dead-Beat Body

Breath is essential to all forms of life.
Without breath, the body dies.
Without breath, creation stops.

- Sheevaun Moran

Without breath we are a lifeless body.
I already know how to breathe, what's to learn here?

One of the things I talk about is **breath**. I say breath and people usually respond by their learned response of shallow breathing. The first thing that you need to learn how to do before you even try meditating is proper breathing techniques. No matter where you are in your journey of meditating – just beginning, occasional or advanced - most people aren't breathing properly. When you don't breath properly, you don't get the best results from meditation time.

If you have the desire to see the fullest benefits of medita-
tion and want to succeed on a long-term basis then it is best to
take a moment and learn this simple technique.

Breath is one of the most talked about techniques in meditation, yet it is also one of the least understood elements of successful
meditation. The majority of Americans deprive their bodies and
brains of breath. We only use 10 to 20 percent of our lung capacity
when we breathe. Our lungs are one of the largest purifiers of
toxins that come in to the body. The fact that we use such a small
portion of our lungs is alarming. Most people have the perception
that because they are alive, breath is no big deal. Everyone says, I
already breath, so I'll skip over proper breathing during meditation.
However, breath is the single largest factor in building the foundation for lifelong successful meditation or even lifelong stress reduc-
tion. Breath is a big deal. I'll repeat: **BREATH IS A BIG DEAL.** It
is the key to our life, our health and our ability to overcome almost
any physical issue.

By the time we are five years old, we have already learned to
breathe improperly. Our parents are in constant states of hurry and
worry, and we mimic their style of shallow breathing. If you hold a
baby and are feeling frenetic and your breathing is erratic then the
baby responds by crying. Remember that your lungs are on both
sides of your heart. Hmm, maybe there's something to this
breathing thing and reducing the heart rate.

I learned how poorly I was breathing, long before I started
meditation. It dates back to when I decided I wanted to be heard at
the back of the room during presentations. Before that, people told
me it was hard to hear me and I felt as if I was yelling when I tried
to speak louder. I took singing lessons and learned how to breathe
deeply and completely and to use the capacity of my lungs for my
words rather than my vocal cords. Wow, what a difference that
made in my life. I had no idea how oxygen-deprived I had been.

You are oxygen deprived too if you find yourself having to "tell" yourself to breathe because you realize you've been holding your breath. We often hold our breath at work or when we are working on something that requires deep concentration. This is a terrible habit and one that needs to be paid attention to in order to break.

When we are healthy, we breathe evenly, albeit shallow, no matter what the situation or what the external condition. The challenge is that because we breathe so poorly, we are not as healthy as we could be. Our body is not supposed to sit hunched over a computer keyboard scrunching our solar plexus and the bottom of our lungs and diaphragm. It is not natural to slouch and then try to have healthy conversations.

Many people say, "Oh, I've been taught to breathe properly during workouts or yoga." I ask, Where is the breath the rest of the time? Breath is meant to be even all day so that your body and brain get the maximum amount of oxygen. Your back and spine are meant to receive all that oxygen to hold you up all day long. Breathing evenly is meant to keep your adrenals from constant firing which is that fight or flight mechanism.

The human can consciously regulate breath, which in turn can regulate body function. We can increase or decrease our blood pressure and heart rate just by regulating our breath. The autonomic nervous system (part of the nervous system in humans that controls involuntary activity - for example - the action of the heart and glands, breathing, digestive processes, and reflex actions) can be balanced just by the use of proper breath. Have you ever witnessed a panic attack? The individual is hyperventilating. By breathing properly, these maladies can be reduced. Sleep apnea is often the result of under-breathing. Forgetfulness is a sign of too little oxygen.

We are more aware of how we look than how we sound. Sound is important because all sound comes from breath. When it comes to breathing, most people use their voice box to make sound, when in fact we serve ourselves better by using our lungs and breath when we make sound. Just as with singing, we need to re-learn to push oxygen into our lungs and system. When we are told to breathe deeply, the air passes briefly into the throat and the body's instinct is to tense up and move our shoulders, thus forcing oxygen into the lungs. Pay attention to the proper mechanics of breathing. Keep the shoulders relaxed and allow oxygen in deeply into the belly. That's the best way and there's more detail later in the chapter. Of course we say what mechanics? Just breathe. If you place attention and specific detail to the way you breathe, life will change, stress will reduce, and you will find yourself laughing more frequently.

One way to get more breath into your lungs is by humming. The small act of humming forces your bodies to breathe naturally. My voice teacher used to have me do these silly exercises of trying to get my lips to relax by inhaling through my nose, then relaxing my jaw, then blowing. This exercise actually will show you how winded you really are. It's a fun way to exercise your lungs and lips, particularly while driving. My teacher had me practice this until I was able to release through my lips for more than a minute. This meant that I was actually receiving the proper amount of oxygen into the deepest parts of my lungs. I was breathing evenly enough so that I was able to release as much as I had taken in. Mind you, this takes a good bit of practice.

Here's how breathing is best re-learned:

1. Sit in a chair that has a firm seat. One that has too much cushion makes this more difficult.
2. Sit with your spine erect. Or as your mother used to stay "sit up straight".
3. It is often helpful to sit on the edge of the chair, so that the spine is more easily straightened. The reason for this is that the

curve of the spine is attained more easily when you are seated at the edge.

4. Uncross your arms and legs.

5. Place your hands on your mid-thigh with the palms facing upward.

6. Place your left hand below your belly button, with the thumb half an inch below the belly button.

7. Exhale everything out of your lungs. For this you breathe in and blow through the mouth.

8. Place the tip of the tongue on the roof of your mouth (the pallet). It's just like when you were a kid and curled your tongue backwards. Note: In the beginning you will feel weird, your tongue may feel tense, your jaw may tense up, and you may drool a bit. This is because you haven't done this in a while. You will get better at this over time. In the beginning, there is no specific place for the tongue to connect to on the pallet, behind the teeth or the middle is just fine. An advanced yogi's tongue, can go as far back as the soft part of the pallet without the ridges.

9. Breathe in through the nose. If your nose is congested then do a few jumping jacks to clear the pathways of the nostrils.
Note: The inhale breath should be getting into the lower belly where the left hand is placed. Then the breath should get into the middle. Lastly, the breath should get into the top of the lungs. It's a three-part process – lower abdomen, middle chest, then upper chest.

10. Hold.

11. Breathe out through the nose. This is also a three -art process – the out breath should release from the upper chest, then the middle, then the abdomen.

12. Hold.

13. Do this several times to get the feel of it. Read the steps a few times and your body will know what to do on its own. This is

actually natural. Try this several times before you move to the last step.

14. For the best rhythmic breathing - breathe in to the count of six and hold to the count of three. Breathe out to the count of six and hold to the count of three. Do this for a total of six times.

Sign up at http://www.SheevaunMoran.com for access to a selection of meditation CDs.

If you are having difficulty trying to do this breathing technique, try it while you are lying down. Just like a baby, the breath will go to the lower abdomen first, the middle of the chest second, and the top of the lungs last which will inflate the lungs more evenly. To watch a live demonstration of breathing techniques go to http://LearnToMeditateIn2Minutes.com/book-videos.html

I've taught many corporate meditation classes and one of the most often asked questions is what can I do to get to sleep or stay asleep. This simple breathing technique can help your body get the rest that it requires.

Be sure that you are inflating the abdomen first, the middle of the chest second, and the top of the lungs last. Your shoulders should not hunch up towards your ears. If they are doing that, then you will want to go back to re-training your body to breathe properly by using the lying down technique. It's normal to need practice. We have been programmed to breathe improperly for so long that you need time to get breathing back to where you started, before you were five years old.

One of the best places to practice this rhythmic breathing is in your car. You'll have a greater tendency to have your spine straight and you have dedicated time built in. Turn off the radio as the music will disrupt your even breathing technique. If you have kids in the car, they will begin to breathe at your pace, resulting in more quiet time.

Another fantastic place to practice breathing is in the shower because you have water, which contains cleaner oxygen and more dedicated time. That's why singing in the shower is so good for you, you breathe and you allow your body and brain to get the maximum amount of oxygen without forcing it.

The objective of proper breath is to be even and consistent. When doen right, you feel much more awake and aware.

7

REJUVENATION: REFRESHING THE FACE AND BODY

"The best and most beautiful things in this world cannot be seen or even heard, but must be felt with the heart."

- Helen Keller

Yes, your face will look younger!
It's possible that you'll have a spring in your step.

Have you ever noticed how happy the Dalai Llama always looks? A very interesting thing happens when someone is happy or at peace within themselves. Their face drops lines of age. The same thing occurs when one is in love, lines and fatigue just seem to disappear. It is curious to know that just a few moments of love and laughter can alter the light of someone's facial features.

The simplicity of proper breath into the body and the organs allow the facial features to soften. Adding meditation allows the restoration of vitality and youthfulness to the entire system.

Stress is one of the main factors for the lines on your face. Energetically, there is a direct correlation between each line on your face and an event or series of events that have transformed your facial features. You can clearly identify a line on the face and its origin through the use of energy reading or face reading. It is said in ancient face reading that your face tells every story - how you act, react, and view life. With ancient face reading techniques, it is much more difficult to read faces that are youthful because they have fewer lines. But creases in your face give character and your reaction will show how that character develops.

For example, the lines on the side of the mouth, sloping downwards, can indicate someone who has a tendency to think more negatively. The lines can also indicate that there has been a tremendous amount of disappointment if the skin around those lines begins to sag in the jaw line in an exaggerated manner.

Someone who has been meditating for years will have eyes that seem to shine much more brightly. I challenged a number of my students, who told me they were having difficulty in their lives, to meditate every day for seven days and see what happened. Not only did their life and attitude improve, their eyes shone more brightly with clearer, much whiter pupils. Ancient Iridology states that the whiter the eye, the clearer the mind.

In sales and customer service, one of the easiest ways to get someone to pay attention to you is to smile, even if it's only a phone conversation. What happens is that the energy changes every time you smiles. Add loving kindness and compassion and there's an energy of peace surrounding the person. When you're the customer and need assistance, try smiling when talking with the other person and see how a positive outcome just seems to appear. Next, include regular meditation and the presence of one peaceful and non-stressed person can truly make an impact on the environment.

One of my clients had high cholesterol and a blockage in an artery, but not enough to require a medical procedure. In tandem with our energy sessions, I requested that she meditate three times a week. After six months of meditating she had the scans and tests run again and her doctor told her that there was no clogging in any of her arteries and that her cholesterol was normal. He told her that she had the internal workings of someone 10 years younger than she did when they first did the tests. She told me that all her friends were envious of how much more energy she had.

Years ago, while traveling in Nepal, before I knew much about the effects of energy and meditation, I noticed everyone using a hand gesture. One thing that was done frequently by the locals was a hand gesture with the finger tips of the left hand lightly touching the middle of the breast bone and nodding with a smile or saying "Namascar" (many know this as Namaste), which means "I salute the divine nature within you". After being there for a while and using this gesture for a few weeks, it became a habit. I liked the way it felt within me, as well as what it conveyed to the other person on the trail and it seemed to make us more welcoming to each other.

When I returned to the corporate environment, I began using that gesture when leaving a meeting. The room always felt lighter more peaceful and positive, even if the meeting had been long and arduous. Because touching your heart to show compassion is a somewhat strange thing to do in the U.S., I began to internalize the comment, while keeping the same heartfelt comment, without the heart center touch. However, I would still use the heart center touch and a smile when I was feeling that a meeting was particularly stressful. In the beginning, I tried this just to see if I could get people to smile. Soon it became a regular tool to help foster a more peaceful environment.

Try this now. Place your hand in the center of your chest and smile.

A very good gesture during meditation to activate your heart center is to lightly touch your heart and smile. You may want to add Namaste, even if it is just to yourself, your spirit, or your soul. This can enhance any meditation experience because as you activate your heart center you become more connected with less overall stress and you may even find yourself taking a breath or sighing.

Every time you activate the energy of the energy heart the physical heart responds. Each time you touch the heart center and smile, you are changing the energy in your body, mind, and face. Not only does this gentle heart center touch help the heart, it helps the lungs and the blood. Such a simple and small step can cause a positive chain reaction in the chemical structure of your being, allowing much less stress and more contentment.

Just the other day we had a student at our center who had been experiencing severe sciatic pain. Her face was very drawn, and she had a dark skin tone. Her eyes resonated sadness and she appeared older looking, with everything in a down turn. I recommended that she meditate every day and use the heart center touching method in her meditation. I saw her a week later and she looked so dramatically different that most of the lines in the lower part of her face had lifted. She said that her pain was minimal and things were feeling much better overall. She now had more hope.

If you've never given yourself a facial massage, other than when you're hurt or angry or frustrated, you are missing out. Because the face shows so much to the world, there are a few ways to refresh your stressed face. A facelift is one way to get the lines out of the face, but unless the attitude and internal conflict has some release, then those same elements, lines and features will return. Another way is to get facial acupuncture, which also works well, but again, unless the inner world and inner voices change, then the lines re-appear. One sure fire and easy way to make any facelift more effective and long lasting is to meditate. Not only do you get the benefit of meditation, but I would suggest that you utilize that beautiful energy that you've brought into your being and softly and lightly rub your fingers over your face. All that beautiful energy is brought more thoroughly into your physical body.

After meditation gently rub the face with your fingertips for a refreshing glow.

I have witnessed the transformation in my own face and body, just through meditation and utilizing each of these tools. Even if the body is feeling tired and the face looks tired, meditation will make it brighter and more alive. It's like shedding the old skin and allowing the body to regenerate more rapidly.

So why not give yourself nature's facelift and begin meditating?

8

IN THE JUNGLE: CALMING
THE MONKEY MIND

Meditation is like polishing a
precious gem, the mind.

- Sheevaun Moran

> *What about all the chatter going on in my head?*
> *A quiet mind is a drugged mind.*
> *How to overcome those circular thoughts.*

Did you ever want to tell your mind to be quiet? Have you ever thought you want to stop all that chatter? I did and I used to read lots of books about how to get quiet. But the best way to quiet the mind is BY managing your mind rather than allowing your mind to manage you. You could use the breathing techniques we've shared and it would help calm that chatty mind. An even more effective, way is through meditation. It doesn't have to be a long meditation, but some form of meditation will be a great start to managing the "monkey mind". This precise phrase describes what goes on each time we try to sit down and get quiet or try to meditate with a completely empty mind. We get a monkey mind— a mind that chatters constantly.

In one of my meditation classes, an older gentleman who had attended class many times throughout the years and had experienced some cumulative success spoke up. "How do I get rid of the monkey mind?" I laughed and told him this is probably the best way to describe the mind and how it will monkey around with us and how we let it. He had tried every form of meditation he could find over the past 40 years before my class and had no success. So I walked him through the exercises in the previous chapters. After the breathing technique, he had his eyes closed and popped them open and blurted out, "This is what it is to have a quiet mind, wow."

Imagine that you are in a technological jungle. OK, not too difficult to imagine in our day and age. Similar to the monkey that swings or jumps from tree to tree capturing all the branches and fast moving images of the jungle, our thoughts jump from image to image, from sound to sound, from channel to channel. In our technological jungle, our monkey mind shows pictures of moving images on television, video and computer screens. In the technological jungle, our monkey mind also hears many noises. Somewhat similar to the hum of insects, the rustling of birds, the bellow of frogs and the creeping of large cats, our monkey mind hears the multitude of buzzes, crackles and shrieks of electronic devices. It is just like listening to the radio, watching television and working on the computer while simultaneously having a conversation on the cell phone. Our chaotic minds are mimicking the same technological jungle that we see and hear each day.

Along with modern technology rarely turned off and our need to be in constant communication each day, add the additional chatter of family, friends and co-workers. We don't have much opportunity for quiet. We are bombarded with new information each day and things are speeding up all the time. It's too easy to turn on music or television for supposed entertainment, while supposedly turning off our mind. This is dangerous because every single thing that we take in becomes part of who we are and how we behave. Remember that like attracts like and images and sounds that we don't filter out intentionally become things that we are going to respond to in our unconscious brain.

If we actually try to turn down the volume in the brain, it's difficult because it's been programmed to over-stimulation. We need to allow the brain and body to have some peace and quiet, something it craves. We can than be much more involved and attentive. Entertainment will come from within.

When we sit down and try to get quiet, one of the first things that happens is our brain volume seems to turn up. It is usually going on about what needs to be done, who you need to talk to, where you need to go and so on. Sometimes just turning off the television or radio makes this happen. We are simply not used to sitting in a quiet room without some type of media turned on. Our brains are stuck in the high volume position. The external low volume button has not been used in such a long time, that it's difficult to adjust.

The point of meditation is not to make the mind quiet because that will always be difficult. Having a completely quiet mind would actually mean we are no longer living. Allowing yourself to experience a quieter mind with less monkey mind chatter will help you to live more, discover your inner workings and reclaim what nature has gave in the first place – creativity and inner calm.

If we just allow thoughts to drift by without dwelling on them then we can have success. Because I was so ingrained in business when I began meditating successfully, I found that I would put my thoughts in a file folder and tell my brain that I would get back to them later. Funny thing is I never forgot one item by using that method and the project was usually completed quicker.

By dwelling on thoughts and going down the trail of where they lead, we are telling the mind, to go ahead and solve the problem. Our minds are amazing. Whatever you focus on, the mind will do. If you focus on not thinking about a pink elephant in the jungle, then all you will think about is a pink elephant in the jungle. If you focus on breath, then the mind will think about breathing properly. Once you are in a pattern of breathing properly, then the ease of allowing thoughts to drift by becomes easier.

More often than not doctors recommend a drug to get to the quiet mind. Their response to any situation is to prescribe one drug or another. This is sad. We don't allow our minds to solve the problem when we are taking something that inhibits our thought process. Our minds are the most pliable essence we have and taking an inhibitor ensures numbing without getting to the root of the issue.

Meditation helps with getting to the root of the issue, any issue.

A circular way of thinking is a habit that needs to be broken. Circular thinking is really just meditating on the problem. Once we do some proper breathing and focus on a solution, any solution, then the circular thought process stops. Circular thinking is just another habit. It's a habit that the mind needs to learn how to stop. So in order to stop those circular thoughts, start with the physical exercises, then the breathing exercises and then focus your attention on a solution. **If you don't know the solution, then focus on the words, "There's a positive solution to this issue", and you will end those bad habits of allowing yourself to spiral into deep negativity or depression.**

One of the easiest ways to get rid of the monkey mind and circular thinking is through the techniques already discussed in previous chapters and using the Two Minute Meditations in the following chapters. By allowing your mind and body to assimilate, we become more efficient. Our minds become more efficient at processing and our bodies become more efficient at healing. You will notice after meditating for a while that, you have more things going on and are able to cope more effectively. This comes about because we have learned how to get quiet. Meditation is one of the easiest ways to achieve a quiet mind. Actually, I should say, a <u>more</u> quiet mind.

A quieter mind is easy to accomplish when you meditate. Getting grounded is another essential tool to a quiet mind. Watch the video on how to get grounded http:// LearnToMeditateIn2Minutes.com/book-videos.html

In the early stages, a quiet mind is easier to accomplish when you have someone there as your guide. That might seem difficult, but there are many meditation CDs out there that will be your guide, I have several to get you started. Having someone teach you is the best way to begin meditation. Also participating in a group that meditates once a week is fantastic. A group setting creates a positive pattern and energy, so that it's easier to stay on track or get back on track.

The challenge is to pick a meditation that works for you. The easiest meditation technique to attain the quickest result is the Meditation to Heal the Body and Heal the World. It is the most powerful technique available. It is a guided CD and one that you can use regularly without boredom. It is the particular techniques and how you are guided that makes this the most powerful CD available. Here is a link to our series that's a great start to your meditation   practices.   http://sheevaunmoran.com/products/cds-downloads/

9

IN THE GROOVE: HARMONIZING THE ENERGY VIBRATION

When you meditate on OM, you have to also
meditate on the gap between the two OM's.
It is by meditating on the stillness that one is
able to experience the expansion of consciousness

-Master Choa Kok Sui

What does energy, vibration and chanting have to do with me?
Do I listen while others are chanting?
Do I try to sound like others?
How do I learn to chant?
What should I do after I meditate?

If you are like most people here in the U.S. you have not been exposed much to transformational or spiritual chants. Or at least you think you haven't been exposed and you'll discover how you've been doing your own form of chanting already.

Chanting can seem strange and make you want to shy away just because it is based on sound and the concept is unfamiliar. The sounds seem strange, the language is unfamiliar and you are not sure what to do when someone is chanting. In fact, I bet you think you have never chanted anything in your life. Well I am here to tell you that chanting as not as unfamiliar as you may think. If you listen to music, many songs say the same thing again and again. That is a form of chanting. If you happen to listen to hip-hop or rap that's another form of chanting. Any time you think repetitive thoughts of frustration or anger towards someone else or have recurring thoughts about what has happened to you then you're chanting. If there's ever been a time where you cannot get a rift of a song out of your head - that's chanting. At a sports game where the fans get enthusiastic and repeat that same words, they are chanting encouragement. Cheerleaders are the ones who help the crowd through difficult times or get the crowd excited through their cheers, a type of call-response chanting. Spending time in church in song is a chant as well as repeating after the priest or chaplain. The southern Baptist parishioner is a perfect example of a person who chants. After a passage is read in church, the parishioner repeats "Amen".

Whether it's repeatedly telling your children or husband to pick up their clothes; repeat a phrase in church, cheer at a sports event or listen to the repetition of a song, we all chant. You have been chanting since you were a child asking questions repetitively. If you were in school and watched someone get into a fight, you might have noticed the kids chanting. You not only chant aloud, but you also chant in the silence of your thoughts. Your silent chants could be about money and wishing you had more or worrying about not having enough. Your silent chants could be about feeling tired. Whatever you do in a repetitive nature is a form of chanting.

Each and every day you chant something. When we consistently say negative things to ourselves, we are chanting. Repeating "no" to your children is a chant. Telling yourself that you cannot do something every time you have difficulty with a task is a chant.

So you have been chanting after all and have been doing it all of your life.

As you can see, chanting can be good or harmful. Repeating negative thoughts or words imbeds them into your subconscious and eventually your consciousness. After you spend so much time imbedding such negative thoughts it is easier to become agitated, upset, argumentative, and just plain stressed.

A small group of people chanting can affect those in the surrounding area. You become stressed when your co-workers repeat the same negative mantra. Your body, mind, and breath are stressed by negative chants.

By using uplifting thoughts in a consistent manner or using other languages that have been using particular chants for centuries, you take yourself out of your head. You can affect a positive change to an environment by simply chanting something positive in it's place. Once you begin to rid your mind of the constant flow of negative thoughts and chants, you are freer to be creative, which fills your body and brain with positive energy flow.

The word chant, much similar to the word meditation, often conjures up thoughts about strange rituals. The sounds are weird and the music is unfamiliar. Most people associate the word with other cultures you don't understand, ritual magic or evil. It is not evil. Chanting is a way to stop your thoughts from controlling you. Once you begin putting positive chanting into use there is less time or energy for the negative chanting and ultimately less frustration in life.

The use of a simple chant changes the energy flow of your body, your brain and even your environment. Any time you have negative thoughts and feelings, replace those with a simple chant and the negativity disappears. A simple chant can stop all that spinning and circular thinking. For example, repeating, "It's OK, It's OK, It's OK, It's OK," creates a flow of energy and space that all of a sudden is not so difficult to deal with. Everything is OK. Another idea I often recommend using is "happy, happy, happy". You would be surprised how you can change the environment in your home, your office, and your negative thinking with this simple chant. Try this one when you're stuck in traffic or at the post office "I have plenty of time".

Some may say these are nothing more than a mantra but effectively chanting is a more consistent melodic or intoned method of using a mantra. I often give my client's little sticky notes with special "chants and mantras" It helps them to easily make the needed shift and get away from their persistent circular or negative thinking. They can get aligned with the healing work they've just completed. Those are good reminders to stop old or lazy habits.

Chanting is a simple way to stop our thoughts from controlling us.

Though it can feel foreign to hear your own voice in some sort of song, you will soon find that chanting is extremely uplifting. Most people are uncomfortable with the sound of their own voice because it is so constricted from what we discussed in the Breathing chapter 6. You may have been caught singing a song when you thought you were alone and it made you feel self-conscious because you don't like your voice. Actually using a chant can help improve your voice and can help all of the muscles around the head, neck and face. Give yourself permission, regardless of how shy you may feel. Chant one of the following words in the comfort of your car.

Chanting is actually a good way to get your body to breathe. And I do mean the body and not just getting breath into the lungs. Some of the most popular chants from India actually bring a specific type of energy along with a cadence of breath that helps invigorate the body and brain. Then there are other chants that bring a specific type of energy that help to remove negative thoughts or energies from your environment. It doesn't matter where the chant originates, the energy behind it is what matters. If your energy is Love, then no matter the chant it will improve the person using the chant. One thing to remember is, if you are going to use a chant and don't know what it means but are drawn to it, use the chant with intention rather than just recite it. Reciting a prayer or chant is only about 10 percent helpful. Actually saying the prayer, being aware of the words and having a loving intention is deeply effective.

I once had a client diagnosed with cancer. She drove two hours each way to my office. During one visit she said she was so unhappy, that she thought she would stop coming. It seemed that she took the trips with her daughter and she constantly nagged her during the entire trip. She couldn't take it anymore. I recommended that she chant the OM word/sound. (OM is a sound of creation and can cleanse negative energies) The next time I saw her and subsequently after that she was happy. She told me that she would use the OM chant under her breath and it drowned out the complaining from her daughter. After about two weeks even her daughter began to lighten up and became more positive.

It's impossible to be angry, irritated, in pain, depressed or unhappy if you are chanting!

When I teach a meditation workshop I play several chants so everyone has some experience with hearing different sounds from different people. I would suggest that you allow yourself to experience chants from all over the world and see which ones resonate with you.

The easiest way to learn to chant is to ensure you have read and tried the breathing techniques first. You'll want to start with your tongue on the roof of your mouth, inhale and hold for a moment. Then open your mouth and allow the air to say the word, not your vocal cords, as you exhale. Fully exhale all the breath and then start again. This will create a much more powerful sound along with being restorative. Try this with some of the following words and feel the difference in your system.

There are several basic word chants you may already be familiar with that I want to share some of those here.

OM - a divine sound of creation that can be used to cleanse energy in your aura and your environment. This truly needs to be a high vibrational chant so that the space is fully cleared. The best one I've heard is downloadable at: http://sheevaunmoran.com/products/cds-downloads/om-the-sound-of-stillness-cd/

Amen - similar to OM, a divine sound of creation that can be used to cleanse energy. Many who are not comfortable with the use of OM use Amen.

OM Shanti - a divine sound of creation that incorporates the divine sound ofcreation and includes the word peace. Using this chant when you are feeling frustrated or there is frustration energy around you is ideal.

OM Mani Padme Hum - a divine sound of creation that incorporates a chant for mercy and compassion that uplifts and opens the energy heart.

Namaste - I salute the divinity within you.

NOTE: The chanting of OM or another word is beneficial but the most beneficial part of chanting to OM or any other chant is allowing the space between the words to be your treasure. The space between chanted words is actually the most precious part of chanting and where the greatest transformation occurs.

There are many many verses of prayer that are used in chanting. Some are very long and some are much shorter. The repeating of the rosary is chanting, using a mala and repeating a prayer is chanting, using worry beads is a form of chanting and walking in a spiritual building, church, monastery is a form of chanting. You are walking in the energy of the many that have gone before you with the same intentions.

Notice it's impossible to be angry, irritated, in pain, depressed or unhappy if you are chanting using positive words? Notice that chanting in your car on a long drive makes the drive more peaceful and traffic will seem to disappear.

Chanting is a beautiful release for your body and your brain. It is not only done through words, music by itself, without a song, can be a chant. Beautiful music that is played in the background is a form of chanting that eases the discomfort of the mind.

The simplist and most uplifting chant you can ever use is "Happy, Happy, Happy".

10

Two Minute Meditation: Helpful Hints for Meditation, Examples of Two Minute Meditations

"Meditation training involves not just one single method but many methods; it's like building a huge airplane. In the same way the transormation of our minds-or setting the right kind of attitude - takes time."

~Helena Blavatsky

Two minutes is worth the time and effort.
Attitude is everything!

Now that you've learned all the basic steps and background behind how to succeed and effectively meditate for two minutes, let's put it all together.

Once you have achieved the benefit of meditating using one of these, then move on and try the next. (NOTE: Each technique can be used for longer than two minutes.) The point is to give you options to select from because every person is different in their likes and dislikes. These techniques can take you and your mind to a better place of peace, healing and creation.

Remember, for the greatest benefit, straighten your spine and place your head on your atlas (on the shoulders with the chin slightly lowered) before starting any of these techniques.

***

Simple and Effective Meditation on Breath

This is the simplest and most effective technique that can be done anywhere at any time:

❋ Take a deep breath in to your lower abdomen, below your belly button

❋ Exhale everything out of your lungs

❋ Sit up with back in straight alignment

❋ Legs uncrossed

❋ Arms uncrossed

❋ Ensure that you are sitting at the edge of a chair

❋ Place your palms on the top of your thighs, facing upward toward the ceiling

❋ Place the tip of your tongue on the roof of your mouth

  NOTE: If you need to review breathing techniques go back to the chapter on breathing. It demonstrates how to breath properly and evenly.

❋ Begin breathing slowly through the nose into your lungs to the count of seven

❋ Hold for the count of one

❋ Exhale to the count of seven and hold for the count of one

Do this for a total of two minutes and you will feel that inner calm. Any time you are irritated this is the simplest technique to get you back to center and restart what you were doing.

***

The Pulse Meditation Method

Lightly touch your index and middle (first two) fingers to the right side of your throat or wrist. Become aware of your pulse.

❋ Using a watch with a second hand, become mindful and aware of your pulse.

❋ Feel your pulse for two minutes using the watch.

❋ The watch will distract you enough so that you are meditating on your pulse.

❋ Work up to the two-minute pulse method without the watch.

❋ Add awareness of the breath to the pulse method.

❋ Close your eyes.

As you work up to the two-minute pulse method without the watch, add the awareness of breath that flows in and out of your nostrils and soften your closed eyes You will then experience your heart rate with more prolonged awareness and you will experience an inner calm.

***

The Water Droplet Melt

Gentle droplets of water cleanse the mind and body. This is not a physical drop of water but an energetic flow that allows your mind and body to have more ease and peace. Having a gentle waterfall, sound of slow moving water or fountain nearby can be helpful during this meditation, but it is not necessary:

❉ Close your eyes

❉ Imagine a gentle rain falling on the top of your head; each droplet is the color of violet

❉ Allow your brain to accept the violet droplets of water into each cell of your body

❉ Start at the top of your head, allowing the violet water droplets to go into your brain, then into your face, neck, shoulders, arms, hands, top of the lungs, organs, midsection, waist, hips, thighs, knees, back of the legs, ankles and the bottoms of your feet.

❉ Allow your mind to guide the droplets of violet light into every space in your body

Do this for two minutes. For those of you able to take your time, take your time doing this technique. This particular technique is great for helping your body and brain to sleep more easily and restfully.

***

Cloud Meditation

If you live in a an area where you have clouds stand near a window, lay down on your back (for this meditation laying down is OK) or sit in a reclined chair outside:

❉ Take some basic cleansing relaxing breaths

❉ Watch the clouds

❉ Give yourself permission to watch the clouds for an entire two minutes

Your only purpose is to watch the clouds for an entire two minutes, allowing for a visual prolonged awareness. Gazing at the clouds is a mindful meditation similar to paying attention to the space or the awareness between multiple chants of OM. This open-eye meditation actually helps the eyes and brain to reset the system and helps the system to be more aligned with nature.

NOTE: You may start to notice particles or globules in the air in front of your eyes when you use this technique. Know that these are particles of prana and are the essence of all life. This is a natural thing to experience when you are relaxed.

***

Incense and Meditation

While incense can be used to clear a space, cleanse a room or change the energy of a room, it can also be used for meditation. If incense is too smokey for you, know that there are smokeless inscense sticks. This also an open-eye meditation technique.

The technique is simple:

❋ Sit about a foot in front of the burning incense stick
❋ Let your mind meditate on the wanderings of the smoke

You can do this for two minutes. It will be effective while bringing you a great deal of peace. Meditating with prolonged awareness on the meandering of the smoke, letting your mind focus on the wafts and wanderings longer than two minutes will bring you an even deeper sense of peace.

Incense is used for clearing spaces and allows the energy of a space to release old, stale and negative energy and thoughts that reside in an area. The most restful scents are rose, lavender, sandalwood and jasmine. These will help calm the system and clear the space.

***

Deeply Awake

Use nature to aid you in a deep awake type of meditation:

❋ Find a tree (If you don't have access to a tree use a photo of a tree.)

❋ Just sit and gaze at the tree, at the leaves. Do not stare as this is not meditating it is a form of escaping. The point is to be awake and aware and keep your wits about you.

❋ Allow your mind to follow the leaves as they move slightly and softly.

❋ As you place your tongue on the roof of your mouth toward the soft spot, discover that your breath is relaxing and slowing.

❋ Take a moment to focus on the energy of the leaves and breath. Notice how you are mentally and physically moving with the soft energy of the tree and leaves.

❋ Give your mind permission to focus on the leaves, the breath and the energy that is going into and out of your body.

Do this for two minutes. If you have time to meditate on the tree, the leaves, your breath and the energy for a longer period of time, great.

This particular meditation is very good when you are feeling depleted and drained of energy. It is helpful when you have done a lot of mental work. This meditation technique is very good when your body has been sick or is sick. It will help heal and restore the system to a more neutral place. You may want to sleep afterwards because the energy of nature is so soothing and calming. Your body may want to rest to allow it into the cellular structure.

Meditating longer than two minutes will bring you a much more inner peace.

***

One Pointed Focused Meditation

We tend to lose focus easily in our busy lives and this meditation technique is intended to help you regain your focus and to entrain your mind. When your mind is harnessed then amazing things happen, along with great clarity.

❈ Place your awareness on the tip of your nose
❈ Touch the tip of your nose with your left index finger, tap 2 times and relax your hand down
❈ Close your eyes
❈ Place the tip of your tongue on the roof of your mouth
❈ Breathe into the lower body, mid-body, upper body very slowly. Use the rhythm of inhale six, hold for three, exhale six hold for three shared in the earlier chapter where we focused on breathing.
❈ Do this sequence for seven cycles.

NOTE: This exercise is NOT meant to be used for two minutes only for the seven cycles. The energy that is generated during this brief practice is enough to last several hours.

You can use this One-Pointed Focus Meditation as many times as you'd like throughout the day. When you are involved in a project that requires a great deal of intense focus or mental energy is the best time to use this technique. Another time is if you have a tendency to be scattered or are unable to sit down and get to the project because of a busy mind. This technique will bring much more focus and clarity to your project and it will allow you to take healthy breaks without losing your train of thought or diminishing your creativity. In fact your creativity and ability to get the job done is much more effortless with this technique.

***

Icon Method

One of the reasons that a church, monastery or sacred place has icons or images of saints and holy ones is to keep the awareness of the attendee or participant, monk or saint in constant contact with those that have gone before them and to keep them in touch with their higher nature or higher self. No matter what your religion is you can utilize an icon in any form as a Two-Minute Meditation.

❋ Stare with prolonged awareness at an icon of your choice.
❋ Do this for two minutes.

This type of meditation will take you away from your lower solar plexus nature, which is one of the reasons for all meditation.

NOTE: Some Indian religions call this the melting technique or meditating on the guru.

***

OM

As mentioned earlier, one of the most effective, yet basic, meditations is on the word or sound of OM:

❋ Ensure you are seated properly.
❋ Place your tongue on the roof of the mouth,
❋ Take a breath in and exhale.
❋ At the same time allow the sound of OM to release on the exhale.
❋ Again, place the tongue on the roof of the mouth, inhale and exhale the sound of OM
❋ Allow yourself to pause in between each inhale and exhale

Do this several times (for at least two minutes) to get an intense amount of energy and be rejuvenated. The best OM sound/chant I have heard was from Master Choa Kok Sui. His vibrational frequency is beneficial on many levels (physical and etheric). OM is perhaps the most easily recognized mantra, one that is of profound significance in both Hinduism and Buddhism is the syllable OM. Hindu and Buddhist people believe this is the primordial sound. They believe that OM emerged with the creation of the universe. Even the Bible states the use of OM.

If you're uncomfortable with OM then use AMEN as it has a similar energetic vibration as OM.

For a download of this CD: http://sheevaunmoran.com/products/cds-downloads/om-the-sound-of-stillness-cd/

***

Music

Music is a beautiful way to meditate and gain peace. Use music to meditate in two different ways:

❋ Focus on the space between music
❋ Focus specifically on the space between the notes of music. Do this for two minutes or more. This will help you create inner calm. Of course the slower the music, the easier it is to meditate on the space. Classical music is particularly suited for this exercise.
❋ Then there's just the use of music to allow your mind to have space for peace and meditation
❋ Listen to uplifting peaceful music

Do this for two minutes or more to aid in meditation. There will be a time when you have become more proficient at allowing your mind to get quiet. For some wonderful meditation music: http://sheevaunmoran.com/products/cds-downloads/soothing-soul-meditation/

***

Sunlight

Sunlight is a beautiful way to meditate and gain peace and mental clarity. The key is to use the sunlight early in the morning or the late afternoon. Midday sunlight is a bit too strong. If you are unable to be in the sunlight or are in an area where there's little or no sunlight then take a moment to imagine the sunlight, while your eyes are closed:

* Imagine a drop of sunlight three inches above your head. Let this be the most brilliant droplet of sunlight you've ever seen or felt.
* Allow it to split off into tiny particle and drip into the top of your skull like a waterfall.
* Smile as the sunlight moves lower.
* Allow it to flow throughout your entire brain, spending more time in the brain than anywhere else. The left brain, right brain, front brain, back of the brain and the middle brain.
* Let it penetrate your face and the top of the spine.
* Let it envelop your entire body, internally and externally.
* Ensure that you bring the feeling of sunlight down through the entire body to the tip of your toes and out the bottom of your feet
* Imagine all you feel is warm and golden sunlight washing each and every cell of your body.
* Spend a full two minutes doing this technique while it is still within your body. Then allow that sunlight energy to expand outside of your body into your aura, or energy body and stay there for a few breaths. Continue to smile.
* Bring yourself back into your body with a smile.
* Pat your body and face after you've brought yourself back.

Do this for two minutes. By meditating on the sunlight for two minutes or more, you are able to connect to the warmth and peace of the day. You are able to focus more on possibility rather than what cannot be done. Sunlight brings restoration to your mind and to your bones and allows for deep healing and inner relaxation.

***

While at a Stop Light

While driving and stopped at a light or parked:

❊ Be aware of the leaves at the top of trees
❊ If the wind is blowing, allow the movement to slow your breathing

Do this during the red light. If parked do this for two minutes (or more). You will gain a sense of awareness for your surroundings. It will infuse your system with air and nature prana.

***

The Flame of Meditation
Using a lit candle, focus on the base of flame:

❊ Focus your eyes on tip of flame
❊ Close eyes
❊ Open eyes
❊ Focus your eyes one inch above flame
❊ Breathe and let go

Many recommend this meditation to get one started on the concentration aspect of meditation. Using a candle for meditation and focusing on the space above the flame allows you to expand your awareness and gain a greater sense that there are many levels of energy. This meditation technique is similar to gazing within the peace of a sunset.

***

Mantras
The privacy of your car is a good place to start. This is the place we've already been singing to ourselves. Why not make the most of your time and change this to a more influential and positive effect by using a mantra/chant. Mantras are believed to lead to higher levels of consciousness. Using mantras for meditation and peace:

❊ OM (AUM)

❊ HUM

A longer mantra commonly chanted, as a Hindu prayer is the
Gayatri Mantra:
  om bhur bhuvah svah
  tat savitur vareniya
  bhargo devasya dhimahi
  dhiyo yo nah pracodayat
This invocation, personified as a goddess, is recited to summon
the universal principle of knowledge.

The Buddhists use a commonly known mantra. This basic
mantra/chant is devoted to creation and the crown chakra –
responsible for higher energies and transformation of lower energies:

❊ OM MANI PADME HUM

Using this chant brings peace to the person and to the environment.

This mantra is said to be the six-syllable invocation to the great
Bodhisattva of Compassion (Avalokiteshvara). This mantra is particularly revered by followers of the Dalai Lama, who is regarded as
an earthly incarnation of the Bodhisattva of Compassion.

***

Contemplative with a Mantra

❊ Choose a mantra or select a positive word, such as peace, and
  say that three times.
❊ Breathe three times.
❊ Sit in the space of just being.
❊ When a thought comes in then use the mantra three times or
  until the thought is gone. Do this for as long as you like.

***

Positive Thoughts and Words as Meditations

Using a positive word as a meditation allows our energies to shift and can change a difficult situation to one filled with a solution and more ease. These type of words help our bodies relax.

❋ Add "I" in front of a word that you are claiming so that energetically it is carried forth into both your unconscious and consciousness. This allows the harmonizing of both conscious and unconscious.

❋ Integrate it into your body (allow it to drift into all parts of your body without thinking about it), which activates your upper chakras and cleanses your aura.

Examples:

❋ I AM
❋ I THINK
❋ I FEEL
❋ I KNOW
❋ I WONDER
❋ I BELIEVE
❋ I SEE
❋ I CAN
❋ I HAVE
❋ I DESERVE
❋ I THANK
❋ I ACCEPT
❋ I SERVE

After Meditation

It's good to meditate but there is a need to pay attention to the time after you meditate.

Remember, after every meditation it is a good idea to come back to awareness of your physical body and mind. If you think about the monks and nuns of a religion and reflect on their daily activities, after meditation or prayer, they complete their chores, which requires physical act.

Gently tap or pat your body, your liver, spleen and kidneys to awaken them back into action. Do some light stretching so you are more fully awake and in your body.

Being grounded is necessary to incorporate and embody the full benefit of meditation, no matter how long or short. If you are always stuck outside your body and ungrounded then you will have a tendency to get sick more easily or have a tendency to have more accidents. The reason for this is that the body is trying to get your attention and get you back into a place of awareness.

If you have a tendency to be ungrounded, this video can help. Here's the link: http://LearnToMeditateIn2Minutes.com/book-videos.html

I always say it's good to meditate, but it's important to reconnect to the earth. Ground yourself so that you can be and do what you are meant to do.

11

Kids Can Meditate Too: Do's and Don't's and Getting Them Started

"When you have patience,
flexibility and tolerance,
you are ready to do great tasks."

~Master Choa Kok Sui

Each generation brings the world children who are brighter and more aware. But, with this blessing comes great responsibility. We need to help kids achieve those greater things. Too often though, achieving those greater things and accomplishments comes at a higher price. Our children are stressed out even more than adults. Because of stress and demand, kids are in need of meditation now more than ever.

Children are enveloped from the time of birth into a world of technology and loud sounds. To a baby's delicate hearing, these sounds are high pitched and difficult to decipher. Just last night, I was at a movie theater and saw a father carrying a two weeks old baby out of a very loud and emotional movie. It is this exposure and experience with technology and sound that puts great demands and stress on our children before they have developed coping mechanisms.

It's no wonder that our kids' have limited attention spans. With the attention of parents limited by all the demands of living and existing in this fast paced environment, kids are often left to their own defenses. It used to be that kids were latch key kids, but today, kids are more likely to pop a DVD in, sit in front of the TV and watch kids. Each image is being placed in front of our children is moving at a faster pace. The result is that kids have hyperactivity, ADD, ADHD, and difficulty sleeping and waking. They are stressed. parents need to meditate, in order to teach their children the relaxing techniue. Many products being developed today get kids to calm down and teach them how to remain calm. There's even yoga classes for kids. While calming techniques can help, regulating the energy of kids is more helpful to their overall health and well-being. One of the key aspects of meditation is for kids to regulate their energy so that they do not get any more energized than they already are.

Children really do want to feel better and more relaxed. Studies have shown that kids, are seeking ways to escape from the difficulties of school, friends, family and life pressures. When I began recording meditations onto CDs, it didn't occur to me that kids would want to meditate. Nevertheless, kids who had experienced a parent who meditated wanted that same sense of peace. This is what inspired the CD *Kids Can Meditate, Too [http://sheevaunmoran.com/products/cds-downloads/meditationrelaxation-for-kids/]*. Kids shared with me their different experiences of a stressed-out mother before meditation, and a relaxed and calm person after. It really was inspiring to me when kids asked if they could meditate.

Since then, I've had the opportunity to have kids in my meditation classes. I even had a five year old practicing in one of my classes. She got it faster then her mom. A simple, effective meditation for kids that I have used in my class is suggested below. It will teach kids how to relax, improve in school and enjoy life.

Let's first learn how to breathe.

✻ Inhale (deep into the bottom of your belly) and hold
✻ Exhale (all air out of the bottom of your belly) and hold
✻ Inhale and hold, and exhale and hold
✻ Repeat, inhale and hold, and exhale and hold for at least two minutes

Breathing this particular way will help frantic energy to calm. It will help kids to focus, sleep better and have more fun in their day.

Let's try a meditation technique.

✻ Place your left hand on the belly button
✻ Sitting up with a straight spine focus on your nose
✻ Keep your left hand on the belly button
✻ Inhale
✻ Hold
✻ Exhale
✻ Hold
✻ Breathe normal from the lowest part of your belly
✻ Repeat these steps for at least two minutes

This process will allow kids to breathe out the stress in their life and allow them to communicate easier.

Let's try another two-minute meditation. (Maybe lead them through this yourself)

✻ Inhale good and happy

❋ Exhale anything that makes you sad, unhappy, mad, frustrated
❋ Inhale good and clean
❋ Exhale anything that happened during your day that makes you
   feel strange
❋ Inhale good and creative
❋ Exhale any words that made you feel bad

After doing this, sit quietly without music or sound and be still. Think about the people who have helped you throughout the day. Be grateful and feel happy.

Two Kinds of Intelligence

"There are two kinds of intelligence: one acquired, as a child in school memorizing facts and concepts from books and what the teacher says, collecting information from the traditional sciences as well as from the new sciences.

With such intelligence you rise in the world. You get ranked ahead or behind others in regard to your competence in retaining information. You stroll with this intelligence in and out of fields of knowledge, getting always more marks on your preserving tablets.

There is another kind of tablet, one already completed and preserved inside you. A spring overflowing its' spring box. A freshness in the center of the chest. This other intelligence does not turn yellow or stagnate. It's fluid, and it doesn't move from outside to inside through the conduits of plumbing-learning.

This second knowing is a fountainhead from within you, moving out." ~Rumi

12

KEEPING MEDITATION FRESH: REMEDIES FOR REGULARS

Whatever you resist persists.

-unknown

Over the course of the past 15 years of successful meditation practice, the need to change things up in my meditations or quest for another method has not arisen. I felt so inspired by the feeling I experienced each day during and after meditation that I never felt bored. I truly like feeling happy because I meditated. This continues to be my motivation. The experience that I have through each meditation is unique and uplifting even if there is sameness. Even if I was watching the clock because I had somewhere to be, I found I didn't need another type of meditation or exercise, but I realize that this is not the case for everyone.

In every beginning meditation class, there would be someone who had meditated for years and was looking to improve their meditation practice. These students all said that just by the emphasis I placed on posture and breathing their meditations are much deeper and their practice is more enhanced.

What I kept hearing from students who were "trying" to meditate regularly was that they wanted something new, something fresh. After doing a particular meditation for a few weeks or months, they were ready for the next step. Some said they needed a fresh meditation to keep them motivated.

Having said all that I know that we all live in a society of what next and let's keep reinventing for the new and improved, but really just look inside yourself to see what is new and changed within you since the last time you meditated. Focus on the gap or spaces in your meditation or between breaths. Allow yourself to have a four minute break between the spaces. Know that this is where you will find the new and fresh. You will learn so much about yourself each time you meditate. You will stop the tiring cycle of same bad habits. Stop focusing on what's next and how to fill the emptiness. Be in the moment. Be in the present.

As a great teacher of mine once said, truth is dynamic and life is full of cycles. Translate that each time you meditate, You are different, thus your experience is different. You will go through periods of needing to push through just sitting down to do the meditation, this is when there's an obstacle that's within you that needs to be changed. These times are truly where the gold lies. It is only when there is no awareness, that you believe it is exactly the same.

Each time you meditate, you want to be in the meditation. Allow yourself to evolve into a higher and new you. This way you will remain fresh and inspired. Every day is different and the need to accomplish something different every day can be a meditation in itself.

Try this; when sitting down to meditate, pause and take a moment to reflect on what solution or end result you want to achieve. Using this technique alone can keep you busy solving life's challenges for the entirety of a life.

Through learning or continuing your meditation journey as well with the most esoteric practice the end objective is awareness and self-mastery.

You can create your own meditations by thinking of a place that you love to vacation or a place that you love to visit. If you are creative, then create a wonderful inner world and envelop yourself in a beautiful journey. (NOTE: Remember to ground yourself after this particular experience.) Many times while teaching meditation, I would ask the class to give me images of beautiful places, a request to rid the body or mind of a situation, and some happy words. I would take the long list and create a customized meditation just for that class. Some amazingly beautiful meditations were created this way. Several of my meditation CDs were created this way. This is a form of dreaming but with specific intention set within the framework of the meditation.

Artwork can be a form of meditation. Whether you are making the artwork or you are the viewer, you can find a meditative place in many pieces of art. You could find meditation in the color within the art or even the brush stroke.

There are the more esoteric types of meditation, for a special purpose or for creating an awakening within. It is more structured and can achieve inner awakenings, elevate the being, and become more spiritual or divinely connected. A few of the more esoteric types of practices are; Kriya Yoga, Jnana Yoga, Wisdom Yoga, Contemplative Prayer in the Christian tradition, Vipassana and many others. By looking at each religion, you will find deep esoteric teachings that can reach the incarnated soul and transform you. These meditation practices are such that you are led by a teacher through aspects of several meditations to awaken and activate the energy centers. These practices are handed down through ancient teachings and offered by ones who have mastered the techniques to a certain degree. The mastery of these techniques can take years.

Again you will find, just as with anything else, practice makes you more proficient. The more you meditate and stick to the practice, constancy and regularity the more you will discover new facets of yourself. You may even discover that you can find more time in your day to meditate.

Freshness is all around us. In nature everything goes through cycles and there is renewal and birth every day and every season. So take a fresh approach to meditation every day and see where the journey takes you.

13

YES! MEDITATE

Knowing others is intelligence;
Knowing yourself is true wisdom.
Mastering others is strength;
Mastering yourself is true power.

~**Lao Tzu**

Yes it is time that everyone, especially you, incorporate mindfulness into daily life. There is no better way to add years to your life, your health, your community. Each time you meditate, your family and community are the beneficiaries.

As you've discovered throughout this book, meditation can mean and help achieve different things to each individual. The objective is to meditate on the right things rather than allow your mind to meditate onthe latest trend or what is going wrong.

Whether you want to achieve a higher sense of purpose, more inner peace, greater connectedness, bliss, or enlightenment, you will discover there are many types of meditation and there are many paths to your objective. Remember the key is to stick with one long enough to gain the benefit. You will discover many types of teachers sharing their form of meditation, but overall, there is one common denominator – to help achieve inner peace and transformation. No matter what type of meditation, no matter who is your guide, guru, or teacher, you will gain insight into you, your personality and what needs to be improved. Through learning or continuing your meditation journey as well with the most esoteric practice the end objective is awareness and self-mastery.

There's even a practice of yogic and shamanic tradition that recommends you place awareness on each muscle, through each movement, throughout the day. For this practice when you walk, place awareness on each muscle movement of the leg. When you get out of your car, place awareness on each muscle through each movement head to toe. This type of awareness can create more grace and charm. What it really does is create the space in order for you to be in the here and now with each movement. It forces one to be present.

Through the yoga as we know it today here in the U.S., the statement "breathe into the pose" is actually meant to help the practitioner be awareof limitations within the body that were created by the mind. Most people take yoga classes for the exercise, when yoga is meant to be much more than breath work and postures. One teacher in India teaches that if you want to do a movement in a pose that you are currently unable to do, then place your awareness on the six other bodies outside of your physical body. Imagine that those six other bodies are actually doing the movement and breathe. What will happen is that eventually the physical body will follow the six other bodies and succeed at what you've imagined. Using this technique, I can now sit in full lotus, which is not possible for me to achieve without this imagining process.

What fine-tuned awareness creates within you is laser like focus or concentrated attention. This is advantageous to anyone

wishing to be more, do more, or just succeed. This type of awareness creates what some call genius.

Most people walk around so caught up in the external compli-
cations of life. This exercise should be given to each person at some
point in their life, so they can be made aware of how each of their
interactions affect others.

Being caught up in life is a sure fire way to lose your
grounding, become unaware and miss a turn you're supposed to
make, or fall when there's no real reason to fall.

Throughout the ages, people from all walks of life have been
meditating. You can too; easily, effortlessly and with deep presence
and awareness. Take your current situation and dare yourself to
meditate every day using any one of the two minute meditations
and see what wonderful changes occur in your mind, and your
body. Here are some suggestions to ensure you take a meditation
break:

❋ If you have to add your "meditation break" to your calendar pro-
gram where it prompts you to take an adult time in, rather than
a kids time out, do it.

❋ Change a common password, that you enter regularly, to something that is a positive mantra, where you will have to type it
again and again and again. You WILL notice many changes.

Where you place your attention is where you'll end up. We
don't usually drive our cars aimlessly, we have a destination in
mind. Now begin to place your attention on meditation and you
will meditate easily. Before you know it people will be asking if
you've changed your hair or what's different about you. Just smile
and say "Thanks, that's so kind," That's when you'll know that the
change inside is showing on the outside. This is your inner light
beginning to shine outwardly.

We have 20 meditation CDs that you can download to get
going and there's no reason why you can't start today. To get yours

click here: http://sheevaunmoran.com/products/meditation-products/

One of the most effective healing meditation you can do to improve your life immediately is the Twin Hearts meditation. This is the meditation that got me hooked. For your free download of this meditation go to http://LearnToMeditateIn2Minutes.com/book-videos.html

14

LEARN TO MEDITATE – OVERVIEW

1. The Myth of Meditation

❋ Can I really meditate without having a completely quiet mind?

❋ Can I really meditate without sitting in a twisted position?

❋ Can I meditate and not feel it's cultish? Most of us have associated the practice of meditation with the image of Hindu and Buddhist yogis sitting in a lotus posture, using strange mudra's (hand gestures) and alternately chanting mantras with complete periods of quiet and stillness for a long time, while away from the world high on a mountaintop in the freezing climes with little or no contact with the outside world.

❋ How can I do this in our culture with the time constraints that I face?

❋ Can I meditate and still be good at business?

❋ Can I meditate and be logical, practical, grounded, successful?

2. How To?

Sit in a comfortable position, with your back away from the chair. Keep your spine straight and your legs uncrossed to allow the energy to flow freely in your body. Keep your palms facing upwards toward the sky and all fingers open and receptive. Place the tip of your tongue on the roof of your mouth – this balances the energy in the brain and the body, and allows both to function more effectively as a whole. These positions are best for two reasons: (1) Achieving prolonged awareness (2) Receiving the down-pouring of energy (from the top of your head) that plugs you into source, spirit, God, the creator, or whatever it is you call this origin of energy current.

3. What is the best time and place to meditate?

According to most books and many teachers, the best time to meditate is in the morning, so you can start your day off with a calm perspective, clearer insight, and inner reflection. However, the morning is **not** the best time for everyone! The key is not the time of day, but rather, consistent practice. Find **your** ideal place to consistently meditate – some place peaceful and away from the distractions of everyday life.

Meditating with a class or group is not necessary, however, it can help to keep you committed to a regular time and place of meditation practice.

If you have decided to meditate on Mondays, then stick to that day. Consistent practice allows your body to access more powerful energy. Also, meditation with a group helps to magnify the down-pouring of energy – seven people meditating together is equivalent to 100 people meditating alone.

4. Exercise and Meditation

Exercise helps to prepare the body systems for the down-pouring of new energy that is received during meditation. These exercises only take a few minutes and the overall health benefits are cumulative over time.

Hatha Yoga's postures were originally designed to prepare the body for meditation, not just as a form of exercise. The exercise routine before meditation gives the body the ability to release old energy, so that it can handle the new energy pouring in. These exercises help to release toxins, energies and blockages in the major energy centers and organs of the body. The new energy is necessary for the body to restore itself, resulting in a more energetic and youthful appearance.

5. Benefits of Meditation - The benefits of meditation are endless – peace of mind, less stress, good health, balance and happiness! And this is possible in two minutes or less!

Physical Benefits – The chemical structure of the brain changes from breaking down to restorative, allowing the brain and body to heal itself. Meditation reduces stress and the toxic chemical load in your body. Meditation increases your lung capacity thereby increasing your body's ability to purify toxins and give you more energy. Meditation strengthens your back muscles and your spine and the muscles around your head, neck and face. You vibrate at higher energy levels when you practice meditation regularly. Your focus and attention becomes more effective when you meditates regularly.

Mental Benefits – Your mind become more proficient at processing life's information once it is properly and regularly rested. You will learn to be the manager of yoru mind and thoughts, rather than your thoughts controlling or managing you!

Emotional Benefits – Peace instead of anger – really helpful with road rage

Spiritual Benefits – You will become more connected to your own spirituality and religion just through these simple steps.

Business Benefits – Less stress. Meditation will help you to focus on one item at a time, even though you've been trained to think that multi-tasking is the best way to get things done. It's really one tasking that is going to get more things done quicker and meditation gives you that ability.

MEDITATION IS FREE AND IT CAN CHANGE EVERY FACET OF YOUR LIFE!

6. The Breath

The majority of people deprive their bodies and their brains of breath. We only use about 10 to 20 percent of our lung capacity with shallow breathing patterns. Breath is the key to your life, your health and your ability to overcome almost any physical issue. A yoga practice is really a breathing practice accompanied by postures, not the other way around. Breath is the most important part. It is important to inflate the abdomen first, the middle of the chest, next, and lastly the top of the lungs. Practice the 6 – 3 – 6 – 3 technique. Breathe in to the count of six and hold to the count of three. Breathe out to the count of six and hold to the count of three. This simple breathing technique can help your body sleep better and actually rest.

7. Refresh the Stress Face

Touch the center of your chest or breast bone and smile. You will find that you are much nicer, easier on yourself and others, and that stress melts off your face and out of your shoulders. For more on this go to Chapter 7 Rejuvenation: Refreshing the Face and Body.

8. Calming the Monkey Mind

How to stop the chatter - what needs to be done, who you need to talk to, where you need to go, how worried you are about, that you'll be late for,and so on. If we just allow these thoughts to drift by without dwelling on them, then we can have success. Instead of trying to push away your thoughts and feelings, let them walk right on by without engaging them.

Do this exercise for a full day and see how much more freedom and space you have in your mind and in your life.

One of the easiest ways to get rid of the monkey mind is by using the Two-Minute Meditations. It is also easier to quiet the mind by following a guided meditation with a CD. The challenge is to pick a meditation that works for you.

9. Chanting

The word chant is similar to the word meditation, which conjures up thoughts of strange rituals - the sounds are weird and the music unfamiliar. Chanting, however, is a simple way to stop thoughts from controlling us. Using a chant can help improve your voice and help all of the muscles around the head, neck and face. Chanting is actually a good way to get your body to breathe. Experiment with chants from all over the world and see which one resonates with you.

How is it that I'm already chanting in my life? How is this chanting affecting my life and how can I change it to make a more positive impact.

Reframe from the words you are using as a chant – things such as "I can't stand it when", "she never", "my boss is so", "this is unfair", "it's just too much work", "it's too hard". Change the words into something more productive - nothing longer than three words. A great example is "I think I can". Now that's productive and that's simple.

Anything longer than three words and your brain can't grasp it - and you'll stop using it.

10. 2 Minute Meditations

I am sure you can agree that two minutes is achievable – raise your hand in agreement so that your body and brain get on the same page? Stop - put two minute interval breaks on your calendar and use it consistently?

Each technique can be used for longer than two minutes, but significant benefits can be achieved by using these techniques consistently for two minutes.

Simple and Effective Meditation – this can be done anywhere at any time:

* Take a deep breath in to your lower abdomen
* Exhale everything out of your lungs
* Sit up with back straight, feet flat on the ground, head on straight, and with your palms facing upwards.
* Be aware of the quiet, the mind, thoughts, air, the tension in your body and just breathe into each of these.

Do these techniques for a total of two minutes and you will feel that an inner calm.

The Water Droplet Cleanse – gentle droplets of water cleanse the mind and body:

* Close your eyes
* Imagine a gentle rain falling on the top of your head; each droplet is the color of violet
* Allow your brain to accept the violet droplets of water into each cell of your body
* Allow your mind to guide the droplets of violet light into every space in your body

❋ Be aware

Do this for two minutes. For those of you who are able to take your time, please take your time with this technique. This particular technique is great for helping your body and brain sleep more easily and restfully.

Sunlight – take a moment to look at sunlight:

❋ Imagine a drop of sunlight three inches above your head
❋ Allow it to drip like a waterfall
❋ Let it envelop your entire body
❋ Imagine all you feel is warm and golden

Do this for two minutes. By meditating on the sunlight for two minutes or more, you are able to connect to the warmth and peace of the day.

Tip of the Nose – while feeling a lack of focus or need to accomplish anything, quickly focus on the tip of the nose:

❋ Put your tongue on the roof of your mouth
❋ Touch the tip of your nose with your index finger on your left hand
❋ Focus on the tip of your nose
❋ Breathe in and out with your awareness on the tip of your nose
❋ Then use the breathing technique for one or two minutes

This is a powerful meditation. It is also a powerful way to get your mind back into focus on what you are doing, as well as a way of accomplishing something quickly and efficiently.

After meditation, it's a good idea to come back into awareness of your physical body and mind. Do some simple exercises to ground yourself so you can be and do what you are meant to do.

Stretch to ensure you are fully back and into your body and grounded (for more on the grounding, please refer to the grounding exercises in the book). Your day is going to be that much more fulfilled.

I guarantee it!

15

STUDENTS SHARE THEIR EXPERIENCES

Students Share Their Experiences

"I like the meditation for Kids. It makes me calm." - Xander, 7 ½ years old

"My mind is happier after I use the Kids meditation." - Brittany 11 years old

"When I listen to the meditation after school I can do homework easier." - Jonathan 14 years old

"With over 10 years in the Psychic Arts field of study meditation has never come easily to me. From your very first class I have been meditating every day, with each day it gets easier and easier. This has been beneficial in my creating so many wonderful changes in my life. I have to say I have received a wealth of information from your techniques." - Vonda

"I wanted to let you know that your techniques have really helped me. I feel a lot more balanced and positive. I ran my fastest 5K yesterday after being in a slump for two years. I just kept thinking, as I ran, about taking in deep breaths and feeling the energy enter my body like I do when I meditate. " - Yvonne

"Since I was a child I've had epilepsy and have been put on medications. I have been taking your meditation classes for the past 3 months and my symptoms and episodes are reduced from several times daily to a few times per week. They are also less severe. I practice the meditation techniques every day and even my doctor has noticed a change. She has reduced my medications and recommended I continue to meditate." - Y. Flores

"Since learning these techniques I have learned to open my heart and mind and receive the love that fills the earth. Although I often felt it didn't exist. This class forever changed my life." - Ilena

"Every time I step away from meditating it seems that my life gets upside down. I'll run into someone who reminds me about breath and meditation and then get back on track. My life is ALWAYS better when I meditate regularly." - Joyce, NY

"My mom is always happier when she comes out of her room after meditating. It seems like she's nicer and it always makes dinner more fun." - James, HB

"Meditation is my sanity. I met Sheevaun when I had 5 kids and wanted two more and she taught me to meditate. Now with 7 kids ranging from 2 years to 18 years old I'd be crazy and anxious if I didn't meditate three times a week and use the 2 minute tricks of Sheevaun's all the time." - Myra, LB

"After listening to your meditations on-line I had to get every single one. I choose one each day and my week is much happier. If I miss a day it seems like there's sand in my engine and everything is clogged up." - Linda, LA, CA

"After taking the basic meditation class I was inspired to help my family and wife have more peace. I've become a much better person just using the techniques in this book." - Jimmy, Florida

"I found these downloads on-line and didn't listen for months. One day I was clearing out my computer files and found them. I turned the speakers on and was so happy I did. My family is happy and much healthier since listening to the meditation's by Sheevaun than ever. We used to get colds and the kids stayed home from school, a lot, and now they may miss two days a year. Our family is much more peaceful. " - Lanae, Seattle

Books
Overcome the 7 Energies That Zap Your Life
Re-Write Your Prosperity Autobiography
Shotgun Shopping - How to Manifest Anything You Want through
the Metaphor of Shopping
The 12 Energetic Solutions for Personal Power

CDs
Transform Your Business with Energy
Tropical Transformation
Woodsy Wonder
Violet Waterfall
Discover Your Divine Self
Reclaim Your Health
Weight Less
Living Wealthy & Prosperous
Clutter No More
Connect to Your Spirit and Soul
Essene Meditations
Kids Meditation
Ultimate Relaxation
The Lord's Prayer - Above and Below
Relationship Recovery Meditation
Soothing Soul
Meditation to Heal Your Body and Heal the World
Master Your Energy Master Your Life Series
****

Please visit SheevaunMoran.com

Published by FastPencil
http://www.fastpencil.com